COCONUT COOKERY

Monument to the coconut located near the ruins of the fishing village of Kamoamoa, Hawai'i Volcanoes National Park, HI. It is situated on a lava sea cliff facing across the open ocean toward Kahiki [Tahiti].

COCONUT COOKERY

A practical cookbook
encompassing innovative uses of the tropical
drupe *Cocus nucifera*, accompanied by
assorted information and anecdotes ranging from
hard data to the frankly frivolous.

VALERIE MACBEAN

Frog, Ltd.
Berkeley, California

Published by Frog, Ltd.

Frog, Ltd. books are distributed by
North Atlantic Books
P.O. Box 12327
Berkeley, California 94712

Previously published in Canada in 1996

Illustrations: designgeist visual communications ltd.
Cover design: Paula Morrison
Within-recipe sketches by author
Plate I: Monument to the coconut in Hawai'i Volcanoes National Park, HI
Plate II by permission of Archives, New College, Oxford

Printed in the United States of America

North Atlantic Books' publications are available through most book-stores. For further information, call 800-337-2665 or visit our website at www.northatlanticbooks.com.

Substantial discounts on bulk quantities are available to corporations, professional associations, and other organizations. For details and discount information, contact our special sales department.

Library of Congress Cataloging-in-Publication Data

MacBean, Valerie
Coconut cookery / by Valerie MacBean.
    p. cm.
Includes bibliographical references and index.
ISBN 1-58394-018-9 (alk. paper)
1. Cookery (Coconut). 2. Coconut. I. Title.
TX814.2.C63 .M34 2001
641.6'.461—dc21

2001033446

1 2 3 4 5 6 7 8 9 / 05 04 03 02 01

*My heartfelt thanks to those of you who have so
lovingly touched my life. I cherish the memories of the many
wonderful times shared.*

ACKNOWLEDGMENT

Grateful acknowledgment for permission to reproduce or quote is given to the following:

Canadian Hydrographic Service for a portion of Chart 3546.

Honolulu Star-Bulletin, Hawaii, for verbatim articles.

Trevor Hall, former student of Douglas College, New Westminster, BC, for his free-association reverie.

The Warden and Scholars of New College, Oxford, for photograph of coconut-cup mounted in silver-gilt, c.1490.

Coconuts on the internet? Visit www.coconutcookery.com.

Coconut serving bowls and a sampling of kitchen utensils made by author.

CONTENTS

FOREWORD

to *Coconut Cookery*, second edition

I became interested in coconuts as a result of my background as a nutritionist and naturopathic physician. For years I had the mistaken belief, as many do, that coconuts were unhealthy because they contained saturated fat. This concept, however, never really made sense because it fit neither the historical record nor current epidemiological observations.

For thousands of years many Asians and Pacific Islanders used the coconut as their primary source of food. If coconuts were unhealthy it would surely have been manifest among these people. However, they have been, and still are, among the healthiest in the world. Studies have shown that Islanders who live on their traditional coconut-based diets are noteworthily free of heart disease, diabetes, cancer, and other degenerative conditions that commonly afflict the Western world. It is only when they abandon their traditional foods to adopt Western diets that these people begin to suffer from the same diseases as we do. Simple common sense would refute the belief that eating coconuts caused heart disease - or any other health problem.

Intrigued by these facts I began investigating the health aspects of coconut products and particularly the oil since it was identified as the prime suspect. What I discovered amazed me. I learned that coconut is one of our most nutritious, natural foods. I was so impressed that I wrote a book titled *The Healing Miracles of Coconut Oil*. In this book I describe the many health benefits of coconuts and I also explain why they have received unwarranted negative publicity. The criticism is based solely on the fact that the oil in coconuts is primarily saturated. However, not all saturated fats are alike. Research has clearly shown that the saturated fat in coconuts is unique and not the same as the saturated fat found in meat. It actually helps prevent degenerative disease as the author of *Coconut Cookery* explains in her Chapter Two, *Coconuts & Health*.

When I discovered how beneficial was this food I began adding as much as I could to my own diet and also recommending it to my patients. I witnessed firsthand miraculous changes in their health. Medical research and my own clinical observations have shown that coconut can improve digestion, strengthen the immune system, help prevent heart disease, stroke, some forms of cancer, and help protect against osteoporosis and diabetes. I have seen it clear bladder and yeast infections in a matter of days.

When I tell my patients to eat more coconut they often are at a loss as to how to comply. In most cookbooks coconut is used only in the baking of cookies and cakes. It was with great joy that I discovered Valerie MacBean's *Coconut Cookery*. Now I have a resource wherein people can easily learn how to incorporate coconut products into their everyday food preparation. I personally found that using coconut added a rich flavor dimension to my meals. It also boosted my energy.

If you think coconut is just for dessert you are in for a great surprise. MacBean provides a wide selection of recipes to make breads, soups, salsa, chutneys, puddings, drinks, salads, and delicious entrées. With this book you can take advantage of the many health benefits of coconut as well as enjoy a variety of tasty new dishes.

Bruce Fife, N.D.

TO OPEN A COCONUT

There are as many ways to open a coconut as there are to skin a cat. If you live in an area where coconuts grow, you have the option of choosing young, or green, specimens. For these you can use a knife to cut and remove a triangle between the three "eyes." You may then drink the water and, with a teaspoon, eat the jelloid substance popularly known as "spoon-meat." The majority of us, however, have to purchase mature coconuts in city grocery stores. For these, I give four methods.

Methods one and two work best if you remove the water first. To do this, wedge your coconut in a corner. Place an ice-pick, or give it your awl (pun intended), to one of the "eyes" and use a hammer or kitchen mallet to drive a hole. Repeat for the other two eyes, and invert coconut at an angle over a jug to drain. At least one hole must be open to the air to allow the liquid to escape.

Method 1: After the water has drained, crack the shell with a hammer, preferably on cement to avoid counter-top damage.

Remove the meat with a small kitchen knife.

Method 2: If you need an intact shell, it is better to use a saw to make an even cut at the desired level and angle.

Method 3: Place the whole, unmolested coconut in the oven; bring to a temperature of 200°C (400°F) and leave for 15–20 minutes, according to its size. The coconut may then be hammered gently around its circumference. This partial baking allows the shell to break with far less force. Use extreme caution to avoid scalding yourself with the escaping steam. The advantage of this method is that the meat will be whole, in one piece, looking very much like a big, brown egg. The brown is its skin or "testa" which needs to be removed. A vegetable peeler works splendidly. The job is even faster if the brown "egg" is placed in a plastic bag and left in the refrigerator overnight. The disadvantage of this baking method is that some of the meat's oil is expelled, resulting in the water losing its delicate, refreshing flavor (but it can still be used in soups).

Method 4: You may try a compromise which is my least favorite approach. Pierce the eyes, remove the water and then use the oven as for method three above. The advantage is that you save the flavor of the coconut water, but the shell will not yield to gentle tapping. The meat is likely to break into pieces, but the chunks will be of a larger size than what results from the first two methods.

After some practice you will become quite adept at opening these gastronomic gems. I usually make a production of it, opening, fleshing, and grating eight or nine coconuts at a time. I shred directly into three cartons labeled Fine, Medium and Coarse. The meat keeps very well in the freezer. and it is so convenient to grab a handful on a whim. If the fun of opening coconuts persistently eludes you, support the national economy: go shopping for the packaged varieties.

The next page illustrates the most commonly used tools for fleshing coconuts.

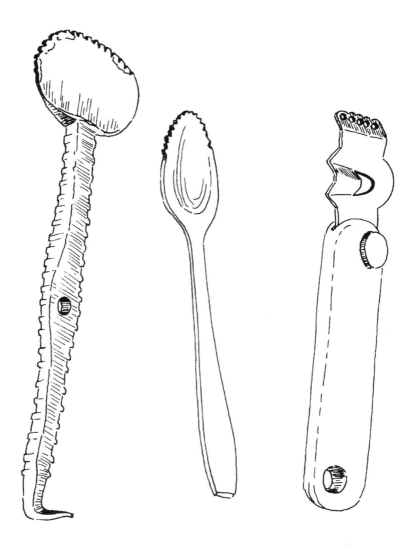

FLESHING TOOLS (purpose-built and improvised).
Left: utensil made by industrial-ed. high school student.
Note the end prong for piercing "eyes."
Center: a grapefruit spoon. Right: a large-gauge zester.

INTRODUCTION — 1

Named reverently and variously as *The Tree of Life; The Tree of Abundance; The Source of The Genesis of Mankind; The Staple of Man's Existence; The King's Blessing, and The Lazy Man's Servant,* the coconut, botanically known as *Cocus nucifera,* has captured the hearts and minds of many of us at some point in our lives.

My own introduction to this magical yet practical item was at the age of eight when my mother, for my entertainment and enlightenment, sang the British rouser *I've Got a Loverly Bunch of Coconuts.* Two years later I saw real ones, albeit little, dried-up ones, at an English county-fairground coconut shy. My mother explained the object of the throwing game and once more regaled me with song and verse. To this day total recall of the wondrous soft-rough texture to my fingertips is invoked whenever I am stimulated by the smell—that most primordial of all the senses—of sickly-sweet, pink cotton candy.

Over the years, snippets of association would occur by such simple events as rubbing my shoes on a coconut doormat; smelling the alluring fragrance in soaps and cookies; wondering at the endurance of old, salt-water-soaked ropes, and the enchantment of a young soldier's tale, told to me, his audience of one, of his life having been saved in battle by a series of coconut water transfusions.

Coconuts: their by-products and the palm trees whence they come provide clothing, food, drink, housing, boating gear, musical instruments, animal fodder, medicines, stationery, ropes, toiletries, fuel, lighting, cooking utensils, fertilizers, tools, personal decoration, legend and song. There are few things in this world which challenge coconuts to match them for functional versatility and universal emotional appeal.

For the past decade, I have played cookery with coconuts in my former galley on the converted tug-boat "Tequila," my present kitchen, on camping vacations in Hawaii—the latter yielding magnificent fresh ones, *"Some as big as yer 'ead,"* and a very far cry from the shies of my youth.

It is with pleasurable anticipation that I have condensed the results of my play and explorations to bring them to you in the form of this book. Because I have encountered many persons who avoid all coconut fare due to fear of the postulated ill-effects of saturated fats, I have included a chapter of my and others' recent research on the subject of coconuts and health. I hope this, and the annotated bibliography at the back of this book, will allay anxiety. I invite you to embark on a new adventure to eat, read, play, and enjoy coconuts!

COCONUTS AND HEALTH

2

When I first began muttering about putting my coconut recipes into book form, the more health-conscious recipients of the news were aghast. In the hushed tones, reserved in the Victorian era for another ess-word, they whispered, "What about *Saturated Fats*?" I was stymied. Who was this fashionable devil, this SaFa Bogeyman? I reveled in the life-giving attributes of the coconut, recalling palm trees gracing idyllic beaches, sunshine, laughter and bright, happy smiles of vibrant people—a far cry from the fears of ill-health and high-anxiety dieting!

I knew that I would have to gather and present some convincing data to encourage intelligent people to accept the coconut for the nutritious and versatile food it truly is. I share my reading to give you information, not to sway your gastronomic allegiances. With the following as *food for thought* (my mother knows that punning is a genetically-determined trait, paternally transmitted), I hope you will look at the annotated bibliography at the back of this book. My own banner reads "Coconuts are Cool."

Cocus nucifera grows in coastal areas bounded by latitudes twenty-two degrees north and south of the equator. There are two exceptions. The first is a district in India where groves are found as far inland as 80km,[1] and the second is in the southern part of Florida, which is as far north as the coconut grows. Coconut water, oil and meat are a dietary mainstay for the peoples within these regions,[2] except for Florida. Map A shows the main coconut-growing regions of the world.

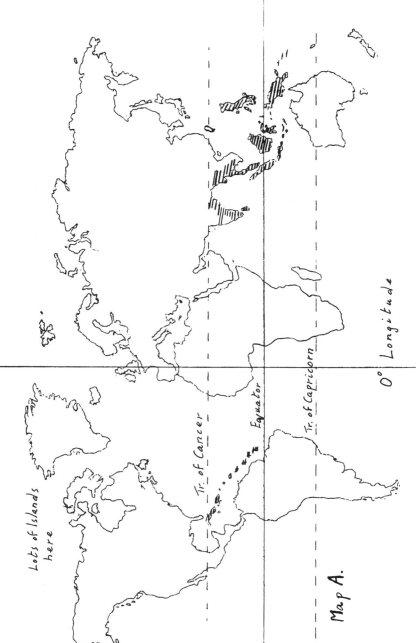

Map A: showing the countries yielding 90% of the world's coconuts and by-products.

Within an hour of beginning my research on oils, I received these contradictions. The first is a quote from a British Columbia dietician in response to my telephone enquiry concerning nutrient values. Her concern for my well-being was entirely genuine, but I am glad she remained anonymous. "You don't *want* coconut. It's terrible. So high in saturated fat. . . . You don't want to use it at all![3] The second pronouncement is from John Finnegan's *The Facts About Fats*. He cites Dr. Everett Koop, former Surgeon General of the United States, who describes the tropical oil scare as "Foolishness . . . but to get the word to commercial interests terrorizing the public about nothing is another matter."[4]

Formal research and political persuasion are emitting topical, conflicting revelations. It is a confusing and onerous responsibility to feed a family with optimum nutrition. Solace may be taken in knowing that there is consensus to one item, even by experts whose philosophies diverge in the extreme: an adult's daily fat consumption (of any kind) should not exceed 30 per cent of total dietary intake, and the child's should not exceed 35 per cent.[5,6] The adult's limit seems to align with the diet analysis of the eight main regions of the world's "long livers" (120–140 years.)[7]

Today's food cautions and restrictions, particularly with regard to saturated fats, are largely a result of increases in degenerative diseases. In Canada, the United States and other affluent nations, the leading causes of death are cardiovascular disease and cancer. Other prevalent conditions are diabetes, multiple sclerosis, Alzheimer's, obesity, some forms of mental illness (particularly depression), and accelerated aging.[8]

Demographic indications are that countries whose populace consumes large amounts of coconut have very low incidences of coronary diseases. In one study of two groups of Polynesians, those consuming coconut oil as 89% of their fat intake had lower blood pressure than those whose coconut oil intake was only 7% of fat intake. In Sri Lanka, a major coconut producing and consuming nation (in some areas each adult consumes as much as one coconut per day), the 1978 incidence of ischaemic heart disease was 1 per 100,000, contrasted with a range of 18 to 187 in countries with no coconut oil consumption.[9] In case a picture is worth a thousand words, Map B shows the regions of the world where cardiovascular disease is reported to be the major cause of death.

Libraries and learned journals are impressive, but another of my research sources makes clear the limitations of believing everything one reads, even from the scientific professionals. Heather Fay M.D. is our beloved and esteemed family physician. She is beloved because she really cares about her patients. She is esteemed because she still makes home visits; she assists in some of her referral surgeries; she shows genuine respect for her patients and her profession. She keeps current of recent medical developments (no easy task) and tells me that, due to recent conflicting evidence, she disputes that cardiovascular disease is entirely degenerative. She also questions the reliability of world statistics. Many cases of heart disease go unreported, particularly in Third World countries. The purpose here is to record that there are various and conflicting views on the relationship between fats and oils and heart disease.

In the matter of health statistics, my own impression is that cultural values play a large role. There is a difference between disease and the experience of illness, and the difference seems to be a matter of perception. For example, a B.B.C. survey for *The Healing Arts*[10] revealed that a Briton typically would seek immediate medical consultation at the first suspicion of a heart problem, but pay no heed to a bruise. A Chinese, on the other hand, would often ignore a heart attack but seek immediate medical advice for a bruise. I think this example well illustrates that cultural interpretations of distress are a critical determining condition for action.

At most we can look at trends, some of which are too dramatic to ignore. Taking this drama into account I have made Map C. It is

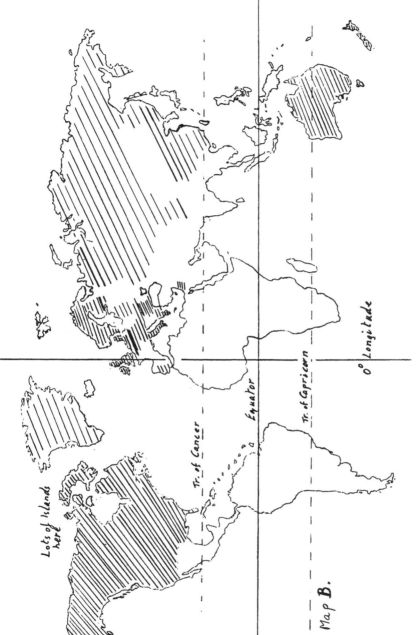

Map B: showing the countries of the world recording the highest cardiovascular disease mortality rates.

Lots of Islands here

Tr. of Cancer

Equator

Tr. of Capricorn

0° Longitude

Map B.

an overlay of Map B onto Map A. While I concur that correlation does not inevitably infer causal relationship, I do believe that an epidemiologic approach to disease analysis is of some merit.

The next section discusses contemporary lipids research and shows how fat is not just fat but a whole series of varied relationships of fatty acids in combination with glycerol. Each permutation dictates a different impact on human nutrition.

Fats and oils are properly called lipids. Lipids are made of units called fatty acids. There are several kinds, falling into three major categories:

> 1. saturated fatty acids (SaFas)
> 2. monounsaturated fatty acids (MuFas)
> 3. polyunsaturated fatty acids (PuFas)

The third category, PuFas, includes the essential fatty acids, or EFAs. They are thus called because the human body cannot manufacture them itself from other food sources. It needs them.[11] Without sufficient and regular supply of EFAs, serious, including degenerative, diseases incept themselves and rampage frighteningly out of control. The EFAs are comprised of linoleic acid (omega-6) and alpha-linolenic acid (omega-3). Most diets contain omega-6 in adequate amounts. In the diets of high-tech nations, omega-3 is most often lacking and can be provided, for example, by the oil present in many species of fish as well as by flax seed oil—the latter only if proper conditions for pressing and packaging are maintained. (More about this later.)

Most fats and oils contain all three categories of fatty acids (a generally over-looked datum) but are described by the predominant one.[12] For example, coconut oil is known as a SaFa because it has only 6% MuFas and 2% EFAs. Flax seed oil is known as an EFA oil because it has only 9% SaFas and 20% MuFas.

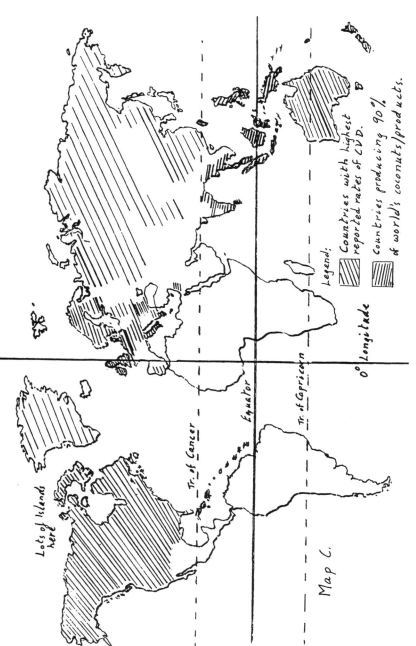

Map C: an overlay of Map B onto Map A (perhaps showing the absence of a relationship between CVD and coconuts)?

Food processing companies use a process known as hydrogenation to convert oils into solid substances with a higher melting point than butter. Not only does this result in a solid food item with an enduring shelf life—a marketing company's dream—but unfortunately it also creates harmful *trans* fatty acids. A recent and more sophisticated method of chemical technology known as "partial hydrogenation" creates even greater amounts of trans fatty acids in the food supply, along with extra toxins. A *trans* configuration in an essential fatty acid prevents its normal functions in the body. It also changes the proportions of good/bad cholesterol with deleterious effects to the cardio-vascular system.[13] Such are the "marvels" of modern food science!

Since coconut oil is assessed as composed of 68%–70% medium chain triglyceride (or MCT which includes C-12) saturated fatty acids, it is easily digested, does not need to be processed by the liver, and is a source of readily available energy (much favored by competitive athletes).[14] Commercial MCT is C-8, C-10 of which 16% is in coconut.[15]

Coconut oil is an ideal cooking medium owing to its high resistance to chemical changes even when heated. It liquifies at a temperature of 24°C (75°F), much lower than body heat. On the downside, it is vulnerable to light and air. Seek, therefore, to purchase a product the packaging of which simulates Mother Nature's. The container should be dark, opaque and airtight, like a coconut.

Coconuts have no cholesterol.[16] In their natural state, they are rich in vitamin E.[17]

By substituting coconut oil for the fat used in most baking recipes, one can reduce the amount of oil by anywhere from ten to twenty-five per cent, allowing a considerable reduction in caloric intake. In some baking recipes one can reduce the fat by fifty per cent and correct the loss of volume by substituting fifty per cent prune purée, sucrose free. For a couple of examples, see Chapter Four, *Breads*,

Coffee Cakes, Pancakes & Cookies. If you are obliged to keep vigil on body weight, use these recipes as a basic guide and innovate menu plans unique to your own needs and taste.

A point for major celebration is this: unlike many fats on the market, non-hydrogenated coconut oil, in spite of being a SaFa, does NOT interfere with metabolism of the essential fatty acids.[18]

The Muse is now upon me to dictate the True Tales of My Uncle Fred as preamble to my endorsement of a couple of products, and no, I have not received one penny in payment.

At a gathering of the Stannard family, my Uncle Fred, the host on this occasion, realized that the fresh fruit salad was disappearing rapidly. He decided to offset the impending shortage by adding four cans of assorted fruits to the serving bowl (a spare, bathroom sink with a well-fitting plug). He added the pears, raspberries and apricots without incident. However, he opened the can of peaches while telling an anecdote and, without watching, poured the contents into the salad bowl. I giggled. The contents were peas. As the group's teasing became more ribald, Uncle Fred got more persistent. "It said 'peaches' on the label," was his pathetic blubbering. Oh, the countless times each and every one of us had to read that infernal label! To put it briefly, Uncle Fred, as in the popular song, "fell to pea-ces." I was impressed.

Six months later, the Stannards' next gathering-of-the-clan took the form of a summer's day at the beach; location: south coast of England. We packed our sandwiches, Thermoses of milky tea (revolting drink), swim suits, sun oils (to facilitate skin-baking), sand toys, water toys, tools for land/sea interface engineering projects and other assorted paraphernalia. We staked out our territory and went swimming *en masse* in the choppy, outgoing tide. Amidst the merriment, Grandpa Stannard sneezed. His upper dentures were expelled to the cavorting wave tops and headed towards France.

For the rest of the day Grandpa's mood was subdued. Ours was not. We had a wonderful time, and it was with reluctance to say farewell to freedom that at sunset we packed our belongings. But wait! What was that odd, glistening object on the incoming tide? Could it be. . . ? No, don't be silly. Some entered the still-choppy waters shrieking with the excuse to enjoy a few more stolen moments. Auntie Nancy (Uncle Fred's wife) caught a set of uppers, proudly returning them to Grandpa Stannard. I had never seen him smile before. But wait! Uncle Fred had perhaps given up the reading of labels. He said, in a most pedantic manner, "Are we sure they're the right ones?"

They fit Grandpa Stannard perfectly. I was impressed again.

What, you ask, has this to do with coconuts and health? A lot. My idiosyncratic family history dictates that I have to witness the peaches themselves, not a label that says peaches. I have to witness the correct fit of the right dentures, not any random set of dentures which happens to be dancing on the wave crests of the English Channel. In over twenty years of teaching I have had to experience every project myself before assigning it to students. Coconut products? I have read many labels, articles, books and product recommendations by most reputable and respected experts, but I can endorse only those which I have witnessed directly for myself.

I have read and made follow-up enquiries of a number of companies producing coconut oil. Several times over a two-year period I have written, telephoned and faxed the most esteemed. The only two companies who welcomed me to see their operations first-hand were Omega Nutrition Inc. of both British Columbia, Canada, and Washington, U.S.A., and Sound Nutrition, Inc. of Idaho, U.S.A. I was impressed.

Aside from their high-quality products, I observed that all three owners share certain character traits. They have a stunning degree of expertise in their respective fields. They are thorough in their investigative pursuits; anxious to implement new findings, and passionately dedicated to serve in the interests of public health. You will find them listed, with details, in *Supply Sources* at the end of this book.

Food quality coconut oil should come from well-supervised, organically-grown coconut groves. It should be processed under strict adherence to healthful methods and conditions.[19]

Much of the coconut oil imported for food purposes is, in reality, of cosmetic quality only and quite unsuitable for cooking purposes. Half-rotten, diseased, and worm-ridden coconut products belong neither in the kitchen nor on the dining table. When coconut oil smells rancid it is because something in it is rancid. When coconut oil tastes rancid it is because it is rancid. Please respect your olfactory and taste senses. Suspect rancidity? Believe it. Throw it out!

When available in an unrefined state, shipped under refrigeration, and packaged in opaque containers, coconut oil is an excellent fat for culinary use.

Butter (including ghee), extra virgin olive oil, cocoa butter, and the other tropical oils (palm and palm kernel) are the only readily-available and reasonably-priced fats suitable, from a health standpoint, for cooking (i.e. heating, especially frying) purposes.[20]

As with coconut oil, purchase olive oil in the form closest to its original state. Ideally, the label should read "extra virgin olive oil." This indicates that it is of the first pressing, yielding maximum nutrient value. Words such as "pure," "light" and "lite" indicate further refinements and are therefore to be avoided. Do not buy oil and fat products in metal containers, as toxins might be leached from the solder.

Many years ago, one of my good friends described his memories of a banquet given to welcome him and his fellow captives after their release from a Japanese prisoner-of-war camp. The buffet was laden with roasts, vegetables, assorted breads, pies, salads, enticing desserts and fresh fruits, the like of which they had not seen for several years. What did these men grab first? The butters, margarines, salad oils and creams. They were after *fats*. They consumed nothing else until the bare fats were gone. With such primordial craving for the substance, does it not make sense to honor our bodies with the purest our purse will allow?

If you are on a strict weight-reduction program, or have serious digestive difficulties or liver problems, your physician may recommend using the medium chain triglycerides (MCTs) separated from the full fatty acids range of coconut oil. Coconut oil is the single richest source of MCTs, which are:

$$C6 \ldots \text{Caproic}$$
$$C8 \ldots \text{Caprylic}$$
$$C10 \ldots \text{Capric}$$
$$C12 \ldots \text{Lauric}[21]$$

Intestinal absorption of MCTs is different from that of the longer chain fatty acids prevalent in partially hydrogenated oils. (For example, Carnitine (a carrier for fatty acid) is not required.) A meal including MCTs creates a high resting metabolic rate which infers a higher utilization of calories, and hence less deposition of fat.[22] One such product of MCTs only is Thin Oil®. (See *Supply Sources* at the end of this book.)

Lauric acid makes up 48.5 per cent of coconut's fatty acids. It is the C-12 component. This is the same acid found in human breast milk and is responsible for the heightened immunity that breast-fed babies have over bottle-fed babies.[23]

Lauric acid is used by the body to make the monoglyceride monolaurin. (As a memory aid, note the root 'laur.') Monolaurin is the fatty acid which fights many disease-microörganisms. These include bacteria, yeast, fungi and enveloped viruses. Research is underway to assess the efficacy of coconut oil in the diet of HIV-infected persons. Other viruses inactivated include measles and herpes simplex virus-1.[24]

With the decline in consumption, over the past decade, of lauric acid, the polyunsaturates, or PuFas, became the oils of choice. PuFas tend to be unstable and, in excess, cause overproduction of the free radicals associated with accelerated aging and degenerative diseases.[25] (Keep in mind that free radicals in appropriate amount are not bad guys: they are necessary for many of the body's metabolic processes.)

There are a number of medical applications for coconut water. One example was the intra-venous application as plasma substitute cited in Chapter One, *Introduction*.

Young coconut water has been suggested for use as home treatment of children with mild gastroenteritis,[26] and intravenously for adults in acute cases of gastro-enteritis.[27] A young coconut is six to nine months old. This is the time-frame for maximum stability of electrolyte and protein content.[28]

Coconut water is better than water for soaking dried fruits as its plentiful amino acids and potassium enhance nutritional value. These properties make coconut water especially invaluable for athletes, physical laborers, invalids and convalescents.

The use of young coconut water ("Buko" in the Philippines, and "Deb" in Sri Lanka) for urinary stone dissolution has also been explored with remarkably positive results.[29]

Due to relatively high potassium content, mature coconut water in large quantities is contra-indicated for persons with serious kidney problems.

For persons who are allergic to dairy products, or adhere to a vegan diet, coconut milk and cream substitutions allow many menu items previously denied. See, for example, Chapter Eight, *Fruits, Pies & Salads*, and Chapter Nine, *Grains, Beans & Soups*.

Treatment with dried coconut, followed by magnesium sulphate purgative, has also been reported as giving ninety per cent parasite expulsion after twelve hours.[30]

By a lagoon on the Big Island of Hawaii I was toying one morning with coconut fibers. A beautiful, native woman strolled toward me from her palm-hidden beach hut. We went swimming together. She spoke to me of the many folk applications of coconut. Her grandmother heated the fibers of coconut husks for use as a body rub. This, she said, rid one of the stretch marks of child-bearing.

Coconut water is also acknowledged, yet little researched, to be rich in growth enzymes.[31]

Indirectly, the common practice of using coconuts as fertilizer is also healthy, as yields from these crops are rich in nutrients. Try a mini-experiment for yourself. Take three same age, same plant seedlings. Place them in three matching pots. Give them the identical soil; have them share a common space and, when it is time to water, give one a measured dose of good old regular H_2O. To the second, give the same amount of water with a dose of commercial fertilizer. To the third, a like amount of coconut water, fresh or cartoned. Watch the results, and check especially for sturdiness and color.

Our skin absorbs oils readily, including the trans fatty acids frequently produced in cosmetics by chemical processes. You learned above how these interfere with the assimilation of essential fatty acids. Why not try food grade coconut oil as the emollient of choice? Its bountiful lauric acid does wonders for the skin. (Avoid applying around the eyes. If it seeps into them, a slight stinging sensation is experienced.) Coconut oil is also a great aid in the prevention of diaper rash. If too late to prevent, a little turmeric powder mixed in the oil is quite an effective cure, and a lot kinder to baby's tender skin that many of the pharmacological products on the market.

A nursing mother would be well advised to consume some form of coconut daily in order to raise the lauric acid content of her milk. Poorly nourished mothers yield milk of less nutritive value. She also should avoid all hydrogenated oils. It has been shown that trans fatty acids consumed by the lactating woman go into her milk directly, and further that their presence correlates significantly with decreased visual acuity in so nursed infants.[32]

Five years have elapsed since writing the first edition of this book. Since then, and much to my personal gratification, I have witnessed my prediction of a grand resurgence of coconut fare. Furthermore, research endeavors have proliferated, continuing to verify and expand coconut's many health benefits and medical applications. In the meantime, nothing of my findings has been refuted; nothing disputed. The future looks even more exciting.

The following may seem like an irksome bit of homework, but indulge me as I offer a brief glossary to elucidate the edible parts of the coconut and to give a grounding of confidence before you sally forth to your kitchen or galley. (It is arranged by logic of information rather than by alphabet.)

GLOSSARY

COCONUT. In service of the interest of being botanically correct, one needs to become aware that the coconut is not a nut *per se*, but a drupe. A drupe, derived from the Latin *drupa, an overripe olive,* is a fruit boasting an outer epicarp, a pulpy mesocarp, and an inner woody shell (the endocarp) usually enclosing a single seed.[33] However, I shall continue to speak of "nut," as the pun on drupe's gravitational proclivity is depressing.

There is some dispute concerning the origins of the word coconut, but the generally-accepted seems to be that it is of Portuguese derivation. "Coco" means "grimace" or "grin," and describes the charming, little, bogeyman face formed by the three "eyes" at the nut's base. This implies a pleasing optimism; would you not agree?

COCOANUT is a mis-spelling, an especially British mis-spelling. No such item exists in this world, and the word probably derives from confounding the coconut with cocao, the seed of which is ground to make cocoa.

COCONUT WATER (also called "buko water" when taken from a young coconut) is *not* synonymous with coconut milk as even many a recent edition of dictionary and encyclopedia would have one believe. It is the clear, but occasionally milky-looking, unprocessed, life-enhancing water contained in the hollow within the meat.

COCONUT MILK is a prepared product obtained by pouring boiling water over the grated flesh of a coconut, and squeezing the milk thereby derived through a muslin or cheesecloth.

COCONUT CREAM is the rich liquid skimmed from the top of prepared coconut milk which has been allowed to set.

COCONUT MILK POWDER is a commercial product usually sealed in small, foil packs. Like its dairy counterpart, one simply adds water to make coconut milk. It is a useful kitchen ingredient as the cook is able to monitor consistency.

CREAMED COCONUT is 100% coconut white meat. It is often sold in block form. The purveyor will store it refrigerated. For a brand with no additives see *Supply Sources* at the end of this book.

FRESH OR FROZEN COCONUT refers to freshly grated (or frozen when freshly grated) meat.

DRIED COCONUT is commercially grated and packaged coconut meat which is dried to the extent of reducing its moisture content from 52 per cent to 2.5 per cent.[34] Typically, a coconut factory will distribute unsweetened fine shred, unsweetened medium shred, sweetened long shred, sweetened medium shred, and sweetened flake (usually fine). NONE OF THE RECIPES IN THIS BOOK USES A SWEETENED VARIETY for the reason of maintaining a measure of control over added sugars.

COCONUT FLOUR is made by extracting the oil from dried coconut, followed by grinding. It is used in a few countries. Its keeping qualities are not good. (One can regard it as a refined grade of poonac.)

COCONUT OIL (or "BUTTER" as a food trademark name for one company) is the fat extracted from the white flesh (meat) or, more correctly, the endosperm of the coconut. The endosperm is either sun- or kiln-dried to make "copra." Coconut oil is derived from copra. Because "coconut oil" solidifies at 24°C (75°F) and lower, it tends to be so called in warm climes, and "coconut butter" in cooler ones. There is a distinction between cosmetic and food grades. Many stores mistakenly sell cosmetic as food grade. Be sure to read even the very finest print.

OILCAKE is a valuable livestock feed. It is the residue after removal of the oil from copra.

TODDY is fermented sap of the coconut palm, and a most popular drink. Sometimes it also is called coconut wine.

COCONUT VINEGAR is the result of failure to imbibe toddy within 24 hours. In Ceylon and the Philippines it is commercially prepared.

ARRACK is a spirit produced by distilling toddy.

TROPICAL OILS comprise varieties of palm oil (African and American) such as date palm oil, palm kernel oil and coconut oil.

HEARTS OF PALM are a delicacy. Each coconut palm has only one heart, the removal of which causes the tree to die. However, it is not necessary to start a crusade against their consumption as the necessity to clear old trees (which produce until eighty years, and live until ninety) is an ongoing process. Nor are the trees carelessly ransacked, for the heart is at the very top and intrepid climbers do not come a dime a dozen. It would be sad indeed for the hearts of palm to go wasted in the process of re-forestation.

SPOONMEAT is the delicately-flavored jelly of the young and still green coconut. The top of the encasement can be removed easily with a sharp paring knife, and a spoon inserted to scoop out the dessert: hence the name "spoonmeat."

COCONUT EXTRACT is a concentrated, synthetic simulation of coconut flavor often used in baking.

COCONUT SYRUP consists of coconut extract, or essence, in a sweet, liquid medium. Concentrates are often used in cordials and flavored coffees.

Here endeth the first lesson. Henceforth, insist your popcorn at movie theatres be prepared with first-class coconut oil. Now, read on. Brandish thine wooden spoon and wire whisk. Cook for good health!

REFERENCES AND NOTES

1. Jasper Guy Woodroof, PhD., *Coconuts: Production, Processing, Products.* Major Feed and Food Crops in Agriculture and Food Series. The Avi Publishing Company, Inc., Westport, CT, 1970, pp. 4–9.

2. Woodroof, pp.4–5.

3. Dial-A-Dietician, Vancouver, BC, March, 1995.

4. John Finnegan, *The Facts About Fats: A Consumer's Guide To Good Oils.* Elysian Arts, Malibu, CA, 1992, p. 22.

5. Robyn Landis, *Body Fueling,* Warner Books, New York, NY, 1994, p. 85.

6. V. Melina, RD., et.al., *Becoming Vegetarian,* MacMillan Canada, Toronto, 1994, p. 113.

7. Joel Wallach, BS, DVM, ND and Ma Lan, MD, MS., *Rare Earths: Forbidden Cures.* 2nd ed., Double Happiness Publishing Co., Bonita, CA,

1995, pp. 191–213 and p. 423.

8. Udo Erasmus, *Fats That Heal, Fats That Kill,* revised ed., Alive Books, Burnaby, BC, 1993, pp. 88 and 320–330.

9. R.L. Wickremasinghe, "Coconut Oil Not the Villain." *Cocoinfo International,* vol. 1, No. 2, 1994, pp. 6–7.

10. T. Kaptchuk and Michael Croucher, *The Healing Arts: A Journey Through The Faces of Medicine.* British Broadcasting Corporation, London, 1986, pp. 26–8.

11. Melina, pp. 102–9.

12. Edward N. Siguel, MD,PhD., *Essential Fatty Acids In Health and Disease.* Nutrek Press, MA, 1994, pp. xxxvi–viii.

13. Erasmus, pp. 102–3.

14. H. Kaunitz, "Biological and Therapeutic Effects of 'MCT' (Medium Chain Triglyceride) from Coconut Oil," *Coconuts Today,* I, No. 2, (1983.)

15. A. Czap, owner, Sound Nutrition Inc., ID. Correspondence with writer, January, 1996.

16. Health and Welfare Canada, *Nutrient value of some common foods,* revised 1988, p. 13.

17. Erasmus, p. 247.

18. Erasmus, p. 108.

19. Erasmus, pp. 144–51.

20. Erasmus, pp. 126–7.

21. Erasmus, p .30.

22. Julian Whitaker, MD., *Health & Healing,* Newsletter. (Self-publication.) July, 1993, p .3.

23. M. Hamosh, "Free fatty acids and monoglycerides: anti-infection agents produced during digestion of milk fat by the newborn." *Immunology of Milk and the Neonate.* (Mestecky, J. et al, eds.) Plenum Press, NY, 1991.

24. Enig, Mary G. "Coconut Oil Antimicrobial Benefits." *Mastering Food Allergies,* Newsletter #89, June, 1996, pp .8–9.

25. M.H. Jones, RN. "Rediscovering Coconut." *Mastering Food Allergies,* Newsletter #89, June, 1996, p .6.

26. William Adams and David E. Bratt, "Young Coconut Water for Home Rehydration in Children with Mild Gastroenteritis. *Tropical and Geographical Medicine.* 44(1992)149–153.

27. V.N. Acharya, et al., "Comparative Study of Intravenous Use of

Natural Coconut Water, Synthetic Coconut Water and Glucose Saline in Acute Gastro-enteritis." *India Journal of Medical Research.*, 53, 11, November, 1965.

28. Macalalag, Eufemio V., Jr., MD, FICS, FACS., "Bukolysis: Young Coconut Water Renoclysis for Urinary Stone Dissolution." *Int. Surg.*, 1987:72, p. 247.

29. Macalalag, p. 214.

30. G.S. Chowan, et al., "Treatment of Tapeworm Infestation by Coconut (Cocus nucifera) Preparations." *Association of Physicians of India Journal.*(JAPI) 1985. Vol. 33, No. 3, pp. 207–8.

31. Child, Reginald, BSc, PhD, FRIC. Coconuts. Longmans, Green and Co. Ltd., London, 1964, p. 201.

32. Enig, Mary G. PhD, Know Your Fats: The Complete Primer for Understanding the Nutrition of Fats, Oils and Cholesterol. Bethesda Press, Silver Spring, MD, 2000, p. 109.

33. *The Random House Dictionary of the English Language.* Random House, New York, NY, 1981.

34. Woodroof, p. 214.

35. The dates on this reference list clearly show a "generation gap" in the popularity of the coconut and its valuable by-products. With hydrogenation, then partial hydrogenation, followed by the dear child of the eighties — polyunsaturated oils — not to mention detergents throughout, the import of coconut dropped drastically. Now we see a timely and much needed resurgence. I cannot help but wonder how severely our food fashions impact on the less affluent nations. What happened to their economies during the time of our abandonment?

ANCHO-AVO SPREAD

Sufficient appetizer for the team

A quick-to-prepare, nutritious spread which suits any type of cracker but is particularly tasty on a crisp rye.

50g	can fillets of anchovies, drained	1¾ oz
1	large avocado, flesh only	1
60 mL	medium salsa	4 tbsp
30 mL	coconut oil, softened if set	2 tbsp

Place all ingredients in a high-speed blender and purée. Can be served immediately or chilled for a couple of hours. (My preference is for room temperature.)

All forms of coconut used in the recipes throughout this book are unsweetened.

BAKED POTATO FILLING
4 servings

Although the traditional sour cream-and-chives filling is hard to beat, if baked potatoes are a frequent item on your menu it is good to break monotony with an alternative filling. A blender is necessary to whip up this recipe.

60 mL	coconut oil	¼ cup
5 mL	hot pepper sauce	1 tsp
15 mL	mayonnaise or ranch dressing	1 tbsp
15 mL	mango powder (or 8 mL [½ tbsp] ground turmeric)	1 tbsp
1	green bell pepper, seeded & finely diced	1

Place ingredients in a blender. Whirl just until a thick purée is formed. Do not over-blend. Transfer to a small bowl.

Serve, or refrigerate and use the same day.

SODIUM LAURYL SULFATE

Sodium lauryl sulfate is a mild foaming cleanser derived from coconut oil.

BARBECUED FIG APPETIZERS

8–11 appetizers providing 4–5 servings

Unless there is a long wait for the main meal I suggest you not make more than two per person of these delectable appetizers. They tend to sate.

You will need wooden skewers. It is also possible to cook these under the broiler with at least 12 cm (5") between the heat source and the top of the appetizers.

60 mL	coconut milk powder	¼ cup
125 g	container soft-ripened Camembert cheese at room temperature with rind discarded	4½ oz
8	large fresh figs (or 11 if undersize)	8
175 g	Canadian back bacon	6 oz

In a small bowl and using the tines of a fork, mash the coconut milk powder into the Camembert until all the powder is assimilated.

Remove stalks from figs. Slice figs in half lengthwise, leaving them joined at one edge.

Place a spoonful of the mash between the 2 halves of a fig. Press together. Wrap a rasher of bacon around fig, taking extra care to cover the cheese-exposed edge. Repeat until ingredients are utilized.

Spear 2 per skewer.

Barbecue on low setting, turning after 3–4 minutes to cook an equal amount of time on the other sides. (If you have a lidded barbecue, the second side may need less cooking time.)

Serve on skewers.

CELERY SAUCE

4 servings

Even a sauce which is based on a can's contents will transform a mundane meal to an elegant dinner. This one is a suitable topping for many strong-flavored fish such as halibut, sturgeon and roughy. (It is not recommended for the more delicately flavored, such as fresh trout and sole.) It is also a pleasing complement to the "Lamb-Stuffed Grape Leaves" in Chapter Ten, Meats.

284 mL	can condensed cream of celery soup	10 liquid oz
45 mL	coconut milk powder	3 tbsp
3 mL	ground fennel	½ tsp
1–2 mL	black pepper	¼ tsp

Thoroughly mix all ingredients together, heat and serve.

CRANBERRY & APPLE SAUCE

7–9 servings

250 mL	dried cranberries	1 cup
250 mL	fresh or packaged coconut water	8½ liquid oz
2 398 mL	cans unsweetened apple sauce	2 14 liquid oz
30 mL	coconut syrup	2 tbsp
60 mL	date sugar	¼ cup

In a medium saucepan soak cranberries in the coconut water for an hour.

Over medium heat bring to a boil. Reduce heat immediately, and simmer for 4–5 minutes.

Add remaining ingredients; stir, and cook over low heat until sugar has dissolved and sauce is warmed through.

May be served warm with pork, moose, or game fowl, or cold as a dessert with coconut milk, yogurt or ice-cream.

Variation: Substitute one cup of dried blueberries for the cranberries and proceed as above.

CUCUMBER RAITA

5–6 servings

*In more than one book I have read that a "raita" is a cool
and soothing accompaniment to a meal's main course.
Less than two sentences later "chiles" appear in the list of
ingredients. Perhaps I suffer from a misperception, but* this *raita truly
does transform a blazing bite of curry to a bearable delight.*

500 mL	yogurt, unflavored	2 cups
125 mL	fresh or frozen grated coconut	½ cup
1	large cucumber, peeled & grated	1
5 mL	ground cumin	1 tsp

In a medium bowl, lightly mix all ingredients together. Refrigerate
for 1–2 hours.

Serve.

CURRANT RELISH

4 servings

*Suitable as an accompaniment to a curried dish or roast pork,
this is an easy-to-prepare relish best made several hours
before serving to allow the dry coconut to absorb the wine.*

60 mL	currants	¼ cup
60 mL	dried coconut	¼ cup
60 mL	burgundy wine	¼ cup

Place the currants in a small bowl and cover with boiling water.
Allow to soak for 10–15 minutes. Drain.

Add the coconut and burgundy. Blend with a fork. Cover loosely
with waxed paper and refrigerate for several hours.

DULSE SNACKEREL

30–36 servings

In my family, for a reason obscured by Father Chronós, a "snack" is something sweet and a "snackerel" is a delight of higher nutritional import. For a day's outing, we find this simple treat superior to trail-mix which tends to impart a raging thirst, usually under most importune circumstances.

1L	loosely-packed dried dulse (or other broad bladed sea vegetable), torn (or cut with scissors) into 4–6 cm (2") pieces	4¼ cups
45 mL	dried coconut	3 tbsp
375 mL	shredded cheddar cheese	1½ cups

Pre-heat oven to 175°C (350°F).

In a small, oiled baking pan, loosely place all pieces of dulse. Sprinkle the coconut. Distribute the cheese evenly over all. Try to avoid large clumps.

Bake for 10 minutes. Remove from oven. Separate the pieces. Place on a paper towel-lined plate, leaving room between the pieces for air to circulate. Allow to cool at room temperature.

Serve as appetizers or package into individual sandwich bags for outdoor snackerels. They will keep unrefrigerated for 1–4 days depending on climate.

JALAPEÑO RELISH

4–5 servings

Ideal as an accompaniment to 'heavier' cold-cuts of meat, this relish is quick to make. However, it is best prepared 3–4 hours in advance to allow full absorption of the beer.
It can be used one day later but begins to lose its punch by the second.

60 mL	dried coconut	¼ cup
60 mL	dark beer	¼ cup
5 mL	Dijon mustard	1 tsp
5 mL	minced garlic	1 tsp
2	jalapeño peppers, seeded & finely chopped	2

Mix all ingredients in a small glass serving-bowl. Leave at room temperature for 1–2 hours, then refrigerate for at least another hour.

Remove when ready to serve.

MARGARINE

15 servings

Margarine can be a healthy item in the daily fare. Here is a superb one balanced for the omega 3 and omega 6 essential fatty acids, with coconut oil to provide quick energy. Use it as a sandwich spread or topping for grains and vegetables. Do not use it for cooking. A mini-blender is the perfect kitchen tool for making this margarine.

Unless you have many mouths to feed, keep to this small quantity as light causes rapid deterioration of the product. It's not too civilized to nag one's guests about putting the lid back immediately!

90 mL	coconut oil at room temperature	6 tbsp
30 mL	flax oil	2 tbsp
30 mL	sunflower oil	2 tbsp

Place ingredients in a mini-blender and mix until integrated. Don't overmix. Place margarine in opaque container with lid.

QUICK SALSA

6 servings

Suited to many types of fish, game or fowl, this piquant salsa may be served either warm or cold.

1	medium white onion, sliced	1
1	small green chile pepper, seeded and diced	1
30 mL	olive oil	2 tbsp
15 mL	cornstarch	1 tbsp
411 g	can stewed tomatoes	14½ oz
60 mL	dried coconut	¼ cup
156 g	can pineapple chunks	5½ oz
248 g	can green, seedless grapes, drained	8¾ oz
30 mL	apple cider vinegar	2 tbsp
15 mL	Dijon mustard	1 tbsp
5 mL	sliced pimientos	1 tsp

In a large skillet, sauté the onion and chile.

In a cup, stir the cornstarch with a little of the liquid from the can of tomatoes until lumps are dissolved. Add, with all the tomatoes and their liquid, to the skillet. Stir. Add coconut. Cook and stir until thickened (about 3 minutes).

To the skillet add 30 mL (2 tbsp) of the juice from the can of pineapple. Drain the pineapple and discard the remaining juice. Add the pineapple chunks to the skillet.

Add the remaining ingredients, stirring gently until warmed through.

Serve immediately or chill for a couple of hours and then serve.

SAVORY CROUTONS

5–7 servings

These croutons enhance green salads and cream-style soups.

875 mL	bread, cubed to 1½cm (½")	3½ cups
125 mL	coconut butter	½ cup
15 mL	garlic powder	1 tbsp
45 mL	grated romano cheese	3 tbsp
30 mL	dried dill	2 tbsp

Pre-heat oven to 150°C (300°F).

Spread bread cubes in shallow pan and bake in oven for 10–15 minutes.

In a large skillet, melt the coconut butter and stir in remaining ingredients.

Transfer the cubes to the skillet and toss to coat all sides.

Pour back into shallow pan; spread evenly and bake for another 12 minutes, or until crisp.

May be served immediately or cooled completely. Store in an air-tight container and use within a few days.

VEGETABLE APPETIZER OR DIP

Yields 2–2 1/2 cups

This nutritious vegetable purée can be spread on high-fibre crisp bread or crackers. It serves as a dip for vegetables or sturdy chips. Don't tell teenagers that it is a particularly wholesome snack, and they will eat copious quantities of something that is good for them.

500–700 g	eggplant, peeled and cut into 2cm (¾") chunks	1–1½ lb
60 mL	water	¼ cup
3 mL	salt	½ tsp
15 mL	olive or safflower oil	1 tbsp
1	medium yellow onion, peeled and diced	1
1	red or yellow bell pepper, seeded and diced	1
1	small chile pepper, seeded and diced	1
15 mL	garlic, finely chopped	1 tbsp
5 cm	piece fresh ginger, peeled and finely grated	2"
60 mL	shredded fresh or dried coconut	¼ cup
60 mL	sour cream	¼ cup
45 mL	lime juice	3 tbsp

Pre-heat oven to 175°C (350°F).

Place eggplant chunks in a shallow oven-proof pan. Sprinkle with the water and salt. Cover and bake for about 50 minutes, or until soft.

Over medium heat in a frying-pan, warm the oil and add the onion, peppers, garlic, ginger, and coconut. Sauté until soft (5–10 minutes), taking care not to burn.

Place the eggplant with its liquid, the contents of the frying pan, and the sour cream in a blender. Mix until puréed. Add the lime juice. Blend quickly and transfer to a bowl. This recipe can be eaten warm, but the flavors are richer if it is refrigerated for a couple of hours before serving.

Procedure Alternative: You can save cooking time by baking the eggplant in your microwave oven. Times vary according to wattage and make, but the cooking time should not exceed 12 minutes. Allow standing time of 5 minutes.

COCONUT SONGS

Songs happen when the heart of man is touched. For a non-coconut producing culture such as ours, I find it fascinating that the theme of coconuts should be so prevalent. Here is a partial titles listing:

Irving Burgie's *Coconut Woman*
Harburg & Arlen's *Cocoanut* (sic) *Sweet*
Harry Nilsson's *Coconut*
Harry Owen's *Coconut Grove*
John B. Sebastian's *Coconut Grove*
Linda Waterfall's *Coconut Milk*
and, best beloved of all, Fred Heatherton's cockney "knees up" *I've Got a Lovely Bunch of Coconuts* (which Londoners invariably pronounce Lover-ly.)

ZOË'S CHUTNEY

4–5 servings

My daughter is a splendid cook and it is my wish to have one of her "non-recipes" in this book. In answer to the question, "What would you suggest for. . . . ?", her reply is always, "Let's see what we have in the garden and refrigerator." On this occasion I asked, "What would you suggest for a chutney to accompany a meaty baked fish or fowl?" This is her result.

60 mL	fresh or frozen (thawed) coconut	¼ cup
398 mL	can mango slices, drained, reserve 8 mL (½ tbsp) of its syrup	14 liquid oz
5 mL	sliced pimiento	1 tsp
30 mL	ginger marmalade	2 tbsp
5 mL	garlic powder	1 tsp
30 mL	lime juice	2 tbsp
8 mL	sweet basil	½ tbsp
5 mL	poppy seeds	1 tsp
1–2 mL	lemon pepper	¼ tsp

Lightly toss all ingredients together in a decorative bowl. Refrigerate for ½–1 hour.

Variation for Cold Turkey:

Omit basil and poppy seed. Substitute 15 mL (1 tbsp) dried mint leaves.

A BREAD MACHINE LOAF

Set this one for the "white bread" category of your bread machine.

13 mL	dry yeast	2½ tsp
500 mL	flour	2 cups
185 mL	dried coconut	¾ cup
4 mL	salt	¾ tsp
23 mL	sugar	1½ tbsp
23 mL	dry buttermilk powder	1½ tbsp
23 mL	butter	1½ tbsp
3 mL	powdered ginger	½ tsp
330 mL	lukewarm water	1½ cups less 3 tbsp

In the order listed place all dry ingredients in inner pot. Gently pour in the lukewarm water and proceed according to manufacturer's directions.

All forms of coconut used in the recipes throughout this book are unsweetened.

BAKED PANCAKE

2 servings

With a filling of ricotta cheese and a coconut syrup top-ping, this pancake brings an inner, benevolent calm to the start of your day. Actually, this dish is properly called a "Bismarck." Whether there is a connection to the historical Prussian chancellor of Germany or to North Dakota's capital city, I know not. I still prefer the name of pancake.

A heavy oven-proof skillet is required for this recipe. Cast iron is ideal.

A cheaper version of coconut syrup can be made by whisking corn syrup with coconut extract in the proportion given below. It is nigh-to-impossible to detect the difference.

FOR THE PANCAKE:

105 mL	butter	7 tbsp
125 mL	coconut cream	½ cup
125 mL	flour	½ cup
2	eggs	2

FOR THE FILLING:

125 mL	ricotta cheese	½ cup

FOR THE TOPPING:

2	lime wedges	2
60 mL	coconut syrup	¼ cup
	or:	
60 mL	corn syrup	¼ cup
3 mL	imitation coconut extract	½ tsp

Pre-heat oven to 245°C (475°F).

Melt butter in heavy skillet.

In a bowl, mix the cream, flour and eggs to make a batter. Pour into the buttered skillet.

Bake for 10–15 minutes, or until golden brown. Cut in half and transfer to two plates. Spread the ricotta evenly on ½ of each pancake. Fold over pancakes.

Add a lime wedge to each plate and serve immediately. Top with syrup at the table.

BANANA COFFEECAKE

12 servings

This coffeecake can be served about an hour after it comes out of the oven. It makes "eco-conscious" use of bananas which are past their prime.

FOR THE CAKE:

250 mL	butter, softened	1 cup
250 mL	brown sugar	1 cup
4	eggs	4
250 mL	buttermilk	1 cup
750 mL	flour	3 cups
30 mL	baking powder	2 tbsp
5 mL	vanilla	1 tsp
3 mL	salt	½ tsp

FOR THE FILLING:

3	large, very ripe bananas	3
185 mL	semisweet chocolate chips	¾ cup
60 mL	finely-chopped walnuts	¼ cup
125 mL	shredded fresh (or frozen) coconut	½ cup

Pre-heat oven to 175°C (350°F).

Pre-grease 25 cm (10") Bundt or tube pan.

In a very large mixing bowl, cream together the butter and sugar. Continue mixing until well-blended as you add the eggs one at a time. Then add the buttermilk, flour, baking powder, vanilla extract and salt. Place half the batter in the greased pan and, with a spoon or your finger, make a ring-trough for the filling.

Filling:

In a shallow, wide dish, thoroughly mash the bananas with a fork until mushy. Stir in the chocolate chips, walnuts and coconut. Turn this pulpy mess into the ring-trough and pour the remaining batter on top.

Bake for approximately 1 hour or until the top is a light gold color and the blade of a knife comes out clean. Allow to cool completely before removal from pan but do not refrigerate.

Serve with coffee or a good-quality black tea.

COCONUT CORNBREAD

9 servings

"Coconut Cornbread.
What an amazing substance!
You can cook it,
Hammer with it,
Put syrup on it
And, God willing,
If Val doesn't cook it
You can eat it as well.
Isn't technology wonderful?"

(Note from a 3-ring binder mistakenly left on the desk of V. MacBean by Trevor Hall, her student assistant (1986–7) at Douglas College, New Westminster, B.C.)

Well, you young upstart whippersnapper! That was then. This is now.

250 mL	yellow corn meal	1 cup
250 mL	flour	1 cup
125 mL	dried coconut	½ cup
8 mL	rosewater	½ tbsp
1–2 mL	salt	¼ tsp
40 mL	baking powder	2½ tbsp
250 mL	buttermilk	1 cup
2	eggs	2
30 mL	butter, melted	2 tbsp

Pre-heat oven to 220°C (425°F).

Place all ingredients in a medium size mixing bowl. With a wooden spoon stir until thoroughly blended. Pour into a 20 x 20 cms (8" x 8") square baking dish and bake for 25 to 30 minutes, or until golden brown.

Cut into squares and serve warm.

Variation: If you wish to use a pre-packaged mix, choose a "corn muffin" mix. Most brands call for the addition of an egg plus milk or water. To create your by now inimitable coconut-touch, all you need to do is add an extra egg and 125 mL (½ cup) dried coconut. Turn your modified mix into a greased square pan, and proceed per package directions. When baked, cut into squares and serve warm.

DATE COFFEE CAKE

9 servings

In Chapter 2, Coconuts & Health, *I promised to include a couple of recipes using medium chain triglyceride (MCT) oil and prune purée as a substitute for regular shortening. Here is the first of these. (See* Supply Sources at the back of the book.)*

An electric mixer may be used, but a wooden spoon and fingers work just fine.

FOR THE CAKE:

500 mL	flour	2 cups
5 mL	baking powder	1 tsp
1 mL	salt	¼ tsp
125 mL	Thin Oil®	½ cup
125 mL	prune purée, sugar free	½ cup
185 mL	sugar	¾ cup
5 mL	vanilla	1 tsp
2	eggs	2
185 mL	sour cream	¾ cup

FOR THE MIDDLING & TOPPING:

125 mL	brown sugar	½ cup
5 mL	ground nutmeg	1 tsp
125 mL	finely chopped dates	½ cup
60 mL	dried coconut	¼ cup

Pre-heat oven to 190°C (375°F).

Put the flour in a medium bowl. Add each ingredient in the order listed, stirring well after each addition. When you have a smooth, thick batter, pour half of it into a greased and lightly floured 2L (8") square baking pan and set the rest aside.

In a small bowl, blend all topping ingredients. Sprinkle half evenly onto the batter in the baking pan. Add remaining batter. Smooth with back of spoon. Sprinkle on rest of topping mix.

Bake for 40–50 minutes, or until the cake passes the clean knife exam.

Serve warm.

GREASING

Reminder: all polyunsaturated lipids become trans fatty acids when subjected to high temperatures. It is therefore a good practice to grease muffin- and loaf-pans with coconut oil.

DELUXE CHESTNUT COFFEE CAKE

12 servings

The second of the fat-reduced recipes, this one is special in both taste and presentation. Make sure that the chestnut and prune purées are sugar-free. (See Supply Sources *at the back of the book.)*

FOR THE CAKE:

7 g	package active dry yeast	¼ oz
125 mL	warm water	½ cup
3 mL	salt	½ tsp
60 mL	prune purée	¼ cup
1	egg	1
60 mL	MCT® or coconut oil	¼ cup
750–875 mL	flour	3–3½ cups

FOR THE FILLING:

250 g	chestnut purée	1 cup
125 mL	dried coconut	½ cup
125 mL	sugar	½ cup
60 mL	water	¼ cup
5 mL	vanilla	1 tsp
15 mL	lime juice	1 tbsp
45 mL	MCT® or coconut oil	3 tbsp

In a large bowl, dissolve yeast in water. Add salt, prune purée, egg and oil, mixing after each addition. Gradually mix in 2 cups of the flour until a pliable dough forms.

Turn dough onto a floured board. Knead for 10–15 minutes, using as much of the remaining flour as needed to prevent sticking. Place dough ball in a large oiled bowl. Cover with a cloth and set in a warm place to rise (about 1¼ hours.)

Meanwhile, prepare the filling. A wooden 'spoon' with a hole in the center is best for the stirring.

In a medium saucepan, blend the chestnut purée with the coconut. Add remaining ingredients and cook over a low to medium heat, stirring most of the time, until the mixture boils and thickens (about 15 minutes). Set aside to cool.

Pre-heat oven to 175°C (350°F).

When the dough has risen, remove from bowl and place on a floured board. Roll to a 30 x 45 cm (12"x18") rectangle. Transfer to an oiled baking sheet.

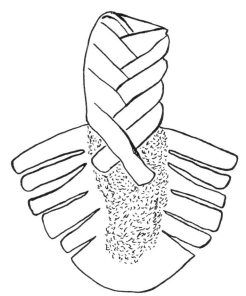

Mound the filling along the center third and cut the dough transversely into ten strips on both outer thirds. (See illustration.)

Criss-cross dough strips, alternating left to right, right to left.

Return baking sheet to its warm place to rise again (about ½ hour.) Do not cover.

Bake for 35–40 minutes or until browned overall. Cool on rack.

Serve slightly warm.

FILLED DESSERT BUNS

12 servings

My penchant for soft, sweet Chinese coconut buns led me to develop my own filling to use in a Western-style leavened-bread bun. The traditional Oriental paste contains ground peanuts. Since I am unable to get past the revolting smell of these legumes (in spite of an acceptable taste), and therefore incapable of kitchen-testing, my own filling is offered in humility. Should you wish to purchase ready-made coconut paste, and language is a barrier, show this to your favorite Asian market people:

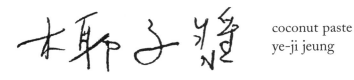

coconut paste
ye-ji jeung

Unsweetened shredded coconut is usually cheaper in bulk at Asian grocery stores too. Ask for:

coconut shreds
ye-si

FOR THE BUNS:

7 g	active dry yeast	¼ oz
125 mL	warm water	½ cup
30 mL	powdered buttermilk	2 tbsp
1	egg	1
60 mL	butter, melted	¼ cup
60 mL	sugar	¼ cup

| 560 mL | flour | 2¼ cups |
| 5 mL | ground nutmeg | 1 tsp |

FOR THE FILLING:

250 mL	fresh or frozen (thawed) shredded coconut	1 cup
60 mL	ground almonds, toasted 1½–2½ minutes in microwave	¼ cup
23 mL	white sesame seeds, toasted 30–60 seconds in microwave	1½ tbsp
125 mL	date sugar or raw sugar	½ cup

In a large bowl, dissolve yeast in the warm water. Add the powdered buttermilk, egg, butter and sugar, stirring well.

Toss the nutmeg with 2 cups of the flour. Add these 2 cups to the bowl, a half-cup at a time, blending well.

Turn the dough onto a floured board and knead for 5–10 minutes.

Oil a clean, large bowl, and place the kneaded dough therein. Cover with a cloth and set in a warm, draft-free place to rise (about 1½–2 hours).

Pre-heat oven to 205°C (400°F).

Transfer risen dough to floured work surface. Knead a couple of times and hand-shape to a rectangle measuring 12 x 30 cm (4½" x 12".)

With an oiled knife, cut slices 2–3 cm (1") wide.

In a small bowl, blend all the filling ingredients together.

With your fingers, make a trough in each slice of dough. Stuff with filling. Pinch dough to enclose filling and place on oiled baking sheet. Return dough to warm place, uncovered, to rise again for 30 minutes.

Bake for 20–25 minutes, or until lightly browned.

Serve warm.

Variation: 4 dozen servings

The same filling may be used in gyoza wraps and steamed as a dessert dish. Gyoza (pronounced 'gee-oh-zah') wraps are made from an exceptionally thin, pliable, almost rubbery dough. On the package they often are described as "Chinese Style Alimentary Paste." The wraps are circular, measuring about 9 cm (3½") in diameter. A 280 g (10 oz) pack holds 40–50 on average. After being opened, they keep quite well in the freezer, and are handy little things to have around for a multitude of leftover applications. You can find them in the refrigerator section of an Asian market.

A bamboo steamer is the designer utensil for this dessert. However, a metal one works fine if you oil the surface before using.

283 g	packet of gyoza wraps	10 oz
1	batch of coconut filling per above	1

Place 15 mL (1 tbsp) of filling in the center of a gyoza wrap. Using a finger dipped in water, moisten the circumference. Fold over in half (so that you now have a moon instead of a sun) and pinch the edges together. Place the gyoza on a steamer rack. Repeat for remainder.

Bring water to boil in a saucepan or wok. Set the rack and steam, covered, for 8–10 minutes, or until cooked through.

Serve immediately.

GINGER-OATS MUFFINS

Yield: 12

Jaggery (or palm sugar) is dark, coarse, and unrefined. It is sometimes made from the sap of palm trees and sometimes from sugar-cane juice. Popular for centuries in India where, to create a distinction as to its source, "gur" is the word of choice to designate palm sap. Although jaggery has the benefit of minerals it nevertheless, like other sugars used to excess, still has the potential to upset body metabolism.

435 mL	flour	1¾ cups
3mL	sea salt	tsp
10 mL	baking powder	2 tsp
185 mL	jaggery (or sugar)	¾ cup
2	eggs	2
185 mL	oats	¾ cup
25 mL	fresh ginger, finely grated (or 10 mL (2 tsp) powdered)	1 tbsp
30 mL	coconut oil	2 tbsp
398 mL	can coconut milk	13 oz

Pre-heat oven to 175 C (350 F). Grease a 12-muffin pan.

In a medium sized bowl, sift together flour, sea salt, and baking powder.

Add remaining ingredients, one by one, stirring with a wooden spoon, but not too much. (Overmixing tends to flatten the outcome.) Spoon into muffin pan.

Bake on lower-middle oven shelf for 45–55 minutes, or until a toothpick comes out clean.

Remove from oven. With the blunt side of a knife, ease each muffin sideways in its cup to allow air to circulate for a few minutes. Serve warm or cool.

SOUND

For as long as I can remember the radio has been, and I am certain always will be, my favorite of the media. I think of it as sound that is so good one does not need pictures.

Every Saturday evening my parents went ballroom dancing, always admonishing me to "be sure to go to bed on time." I never did. It was my right, if not my rite. I therefore have fond memories, as a child growing up in England, of skin-tingling sensation as I sat alone, blanket hugged tightly around me, listening to spell-binding mysteries narrated by the deep, chesty voice which pedantically announced "THIS . . . is . . . your . . . Armchair . . . Detective." Then there were Sunday mornings of wild, abandoned dance to the music of marching bands. Such bliss! To this day I have never bothered to own a television set.

Imagine my pleasure when, in March 2001, I was tracked-down by the B.B.C. to be invited to air live on a Radio World Service program about coconuts. (Imagine also their surprise upon learning I was not in Canada, but happened to be just up the road, clearing the old family home in readiness for sale.) I visited the studio in person. The staff enthusiasm for their work was infectious. Remember, this was a studio, not a kitchen, yet *in situ* they prepared four of the dishes from *Coconut Cookery*. Sound so good, you could taste it too.

After the broadcast I visited the B.B.C. museum next door. During my hour of reveried browsing it was with a surge of pure, childlike delight that I learned the sound effects of horses' hooves were created by . . . you guessed it, coconuts! This minutiae of discovery brought my day to a satisfying, almost magical, completion. All felt so very right with my world.

HINT-OF-ALMOND BREAD

makes 3 loaves

Rising–time and kneading are not necessary with this baking powder bread. I use the loaf/cake pan size: 20.3 x 9.8 x 6.4cm (8 x 3⅞ x 2½"), but if you prefer a larger size pan, this recipe will make 2 instead of 3 loaves.

5	eggs	5
185 mL	MCT® or olive oil	¾ cup
375 mL	sugar	1½ cups
500 mL	dried coconut	2 cups
60 mL	ground almonds	¼ cup
30 mL	lime juice	2 tbsp
30 mL	baking powder	2 tbsp
3 mL	salt	½ tsp
10 mL	ground nutmeg	2 tsp
875 mL	flour	3½ cups
310 mL	buttermilk	1¼ cups

Pre-heat oven to 165°C (325°F). Grease 3 loaf pans.

In a large bowl, cream together the first three ingredients. Add the next three and cream. Add the next three and do likewise. Finally, mix in the flour and buttermilk alternately.

Pour into loaf pans. Bake for 1 hour. Remove from pans and cool on wire rack.

This is a textured bread needing little adornment. It's great with just butter or cream cheese, and even better with a dollop of first-class marmalade for that certain *je ne sais quoi*. Indulgence!

LINZOID SANDWICH COOKIES

16 servings

With these linzoids, one cookie is truly one serving. They are large, thick, dense and satisfying. They go better with coffee than tea (a rare circumstance in my opinion).

340 g	butter, softened	¾ lb
250 mL	confectioner's sugar	1 cup
1	egg	1
250 mL	cornstarch	1 cup
500 mL	flour	2 cups
250 mL	ground almonds	1 cup
250 mL	dried coconut, fine shred	1 cup
185 mL	raspberry jam or spread	¾ cup

Pre-heat oven to 165°C (325°F).

In a large bowl cream butter and sugar. Add egg and mix. Add cornstarch and mix until batter has a light, fluffy "bounce."

One at a time, add the flour, almonds and coconut, blending after each addition.

At this point there is a cook's choice. Option A is to cover bowl and chill in refrigerator for 5 hours and then roll out dough; or Option B is to place uncovered bowl in freezer for 20–23 minutes and then press dough flat.

Roll or press dough to ½ cm (¼") thickness. Use round cookie cutter about 7 cm (2½") diameter. The dough will yield 32 singles of this size. Arrange on 2 cookie sheets. Bake for 15–20 minutes, or until lightly and evenly browned.

Remove. Spread half of the cookies with jam. Make into sandwiches with remaining cookies. Press each one lightly so they'll stick together. Cool on wire rack.

Serve.

MACAROONS

16–18 servings

125 mL	flour	½ cup	
625 mL	dried coconut	2½ cups	
1 mL	salt	⅛ tsp	
185 mL	evaporated milk	¾ cup	
125 mL	sugar	½ cup	
8 mL	vanilla	½ tbsp	

Pre-heat oven to 180°C (350°F).

In a medium bowl mix all ingredients together.

With your hands make patties 6 cm (2½") in diameter. Place on oiled cookie sheet. Bake for 20 minutes or until dark golden.

Remove from cookie sheet immediately. Air on wire rack.

Serve when cool.

SOLE PROPRIETOR MINI DATE BREADS

7–9 servings

This is the answer to a slow-eater's prayer upon sensing the aroma of baking bread: one's personal, allocated serving, entire unto itself.

1	loaf frozen bread dough, white or whole wheat	1
125 mL	dates, chopped very fine	½ cup
125 mL	dried coconut	½ cup
1	egg-white	1
3 mL	ground nutmeg	½ tsp

Liberally oil a sheet of aluminum foil which is a little longer than your cookie sheet. Place the frozen dough upon it and leave for an hour at room temperature.

With a sharp, oiled knife, cut the partially thawed loaf in ½ cm (¼") slices (or a little wider if the process makes a complete mess). With your fingers, pat and stretch the dough into patties about 8 cms (3") in diameter. Whenever you set down the dough, be sure to place it on the oiled sheet to avoid sticking.

In the center of half of the patties, place a small mound of chopped dates followed by an equal amount of the coconut.

Cover each one with a remaining pattie, and press the edges together firmly, making a decorative, fluted edge with thumb prints.

With a sharp, oiled knife, cross-hatch the tops of the patties which are now "mini-breads."

Brush the tops with the egg-white, and sprinkle nutmeg overall.

Slide the sheet of aluminum foil onto the cookie sheet, and arrange the breads so that they have at least two-fingers' width between them. (They will "rise" laterally as well as vertically.) Leave in a warmish area for two to three hours. Pre-heat oven to 175°C (350°F). Place cookie sheet in oven for 18 minutes. Remove breads from sheet immediately, using a spatula, and allow to cool a little on a rack.

Serve slightly-warm, either "as-is" or, even better, spread with Neufchâtel cheese.

ALCOHOL

Western application of the coconut for alcoholic beverages is most often to combine its milk with another distillation product, such as rum, *vis.* piña colada. The Brazilians boast a traditional long-drink, *Batida de Côco,* ("Coconut Milkshake") which consists of coconut, alcohol, ice, and milk in correct proportions.

By contrast, the peoples of coconut-growing regions have developed several alcoholic beverages wherein coconut is of the essence.

When cut, the flower shoots or blossoms of the coconut palm relinquish a liquid known as "toddy" (or "tuba" in some parts of the world). The liquid commonly is drunk by indigenous peoples. Toddy also ferments, usually of its own accord, yielding palm wine —the most common alcoholic drink in some regions. By distillation, palm wine can be made into a liquor known as "arrack."

These drinks are nigh-to-impossible to obtain in the New World, not for reason of being illicit, but because they are largely unknown, and therefore undemanded.

WHISPERS OF PASSION

25 servings

Lighter than macaroons, more substantial than abstractions, these Whispers of Passion *need no* raison d'être. *They make a perfect Old World accompaniment to a glass of sherry. One practical note: you will need a sheet of baker's parchment paper.*

3	egg whites at room temperature	3
3 mL	rosewater	½ tsp
1–2 mL	salt	¼ tsp
185 mL	sugar	¾ cup
375 mL	dried coconut	1½ cups

Pre-heat oven to 165°C (325°F). Line a cookie sheet with parchment.

In a medium bowl beat egg whites, rosewater and salt until slightly stiff. Gradually add sugar, beating until firm peaks form. Blend in coconut.

Place small balls (smaller than golf balls) at 4 cm (1½") intervals on the parchment-lined cookie sheet.

Oven-bake for 20 minutes. Leave on baker's paper to cool.

Transfer to a plate and serve.

AVOCADO &
LEMON CURD CAKE

16 servings

If avocado on sweet cake evokes Heavens-to-Betsy exclamations in your household, by all means substitute two sliced kiwis. On the other hand, are you not a bit intrigued to try it "Just once"?

A 3.5L (13" x 9") baking pan or two 19 cm (7½") square ones placed side by side, is best for this purpose. (Lemon curd is also known as lemon spread in the United States.)

515 g	yellow cake mix	18 oz
250 mL	lemon curd	8 oz
450 g	creamy vanilla frosting	16 oz
250 mL	dried coconut	1 cup
1	avocado, peeled and sliced	1

Bake cake according to directions on package. Allow to cool completely. Place on serving platter.

Spread the lemon curd in a thick, even layer on top of the cake.

In a separate bowl stir the coconut and frosting until well mixed. Spread a thick layer on the sides of the cake, bringing the frosting a little above the level of the top. Carefully mark out the squares on top and place an avocado slice on each one. Cut and serve.

A tropical coffee-and-cookies-in-bed platter. Thematic accoutrements made by author from parsnips and a green bell pepper.

BAKED HAWAII

4 servings

Coconut half-shells look so exotic on presentation that one is free to take all the preparation short-cuts possible. To stabilize the half shells in the oven, place them atop some sort of metal ring or holding device. Suggestions include shallow, empty cat-food, tuna or salmon cans, or large muffin pans. If you are more at home in the garage than kitchen, adjustable hose clamps are an excellent choice. For the table it is a simple matter to improvise a decorative support ring from a half-knotted, colorful napkin.

The coconut meat left in the shells during baking imparts a rich flavor to the pudding.

4	small coconut half-shells with meat	4
85 g	packet instant vanilla pudding	3 oz
125 mL	dried coconut	½ cup
1	meringue instant mix for 1 pie	1

Optional at-table topping: **Whipped cream**

Pre-heat oven to temperature stated on packet of meringue mix.

Prepare the vanilla pudding per package directions. As soon as it is well blended, stir in coconut. Transfer immediately to coconut half-shells, leaving space at top for meringue. Allow to set.

Follow directions for meringue mix. Divide into 4 equal amounts and spoon onto puddings, arranging little center peaks. Bake according to directions.

Serve directly from oven.

BUTTERNUT SQUASH PUDDING

5–7 servings

As dessert or snack, this is an unusual and nutritious victual to challenge the staid palate.

680–900 g	butternut squash, peeled, seeded & cut into cubes	1½–2 lbs
2	eggs	2
15 mL	cornstarch	1 tbsp
60 mL	honey	¼ cup
3 mL	ground nutmeg	½ tsp
8 mL	vanilla	½ tbsp
400 mL	coconut milk	13.5 oz

Place butternut squash in a saucepan, cover with water and bring to boil. Reduce heat and simmer for 15 minutes, or until slightly soft. Drain. Transfer to a mixing bowl and set aside.

Place the eggs in the saucepan and whisk lightly. Add the remaining ingredients. Cook over medium heat for 15 minutes, stirring constantly.

Pour into the bowl with the squash. Blend until smooth. Return to saucepan and stir for another 5 minutes over medium heat.

Put into serving dishes and allow to cool at room temperature for 15 minutes.

Serve warm or refrigerate for 2–4 hours and serve cold.

CASSAVA PUDDING

10 servings

This recipe is usually served as dessert, but I find that, unless the main course has been half a lettuce leaf, it is too heavy after a meal and, to my taste, makes an ideal break-fast. The grated cassava takes two packets of 454g (16 oz) each.

900 g	frozen, grated cassava, thawed to room temperature (2 packets)	2 lb
250 mL	dried coconut	1 cup
175 mL	sugar	1½ cups
60 mL	butter, melted	¼ cup
5 mL	ground ginger	1 tsp
5 mL	ground nutmeg	1 tsp
5 mL	imitation rum extract	1 tsp
3	eggs	3
500 mL	buttermilk	2 cups

Pre-heat oven to 190°C (375°F).

In a large bowl and with a wooden spoon, mix all but the last two ingredients. In a separate bowl, whisk the eggs until fluffy. Stir eggs into the cassava mix. Add the buttermilk and blend well. Turn into a square, greased 2L (8" x 8" x 2") glass oven-dish, and bake until light, golden brown, about 1 hour.

Serve warm. Some like a little half-and-half poured on the side.

COCOA CAKE

14 servings

Cats go a bit crazy to get a chunk of this one, but it is not good for them. Catnip effects aside, this perfectly respectable, conservative cake is well-liked by solid citizens with an honest penchant for things chocolate. (Unless the weather is hot, the cake will keep a few days without refrigeration if placed in a cake tin with a well-fitting lid.)

375 mL	flour	1½ cups
280 mL	pure cocoa powder	1 cup + 2 tbsp
8 mL	baking powder	1½ tsp
250 mL	butter, softened	1 cup
625 mL	sugar	2½ cups
4	eggs	4
5 mL	rose water	1 tsp
10 mL	vanilla	2 tsp
250 mL	coconut milk	1 cup
45 mL	water	3 tbsp

Pre-heat oven to 175°C (350°F). Butter and flour a bundt or tube pan.

In a large bowl sift together the flour, cocoa, and baking powder. Set aside.

In a medium bowl cream the butter and sugar. Add the rose water, vanilla extract and eggs singly, mixing after each addition.

Slowly pour the mix into the dry ingredients, stirring its contents continuously.

Add the coconut milk and water, a small portion at a time, stirring until a smooth batter forms.

Transfer batter to the bundt pan, and bake for 1½ hours or until a knife inserted into the cake comes out clean. Cool in pan at room temperature for half-an-hour. Remove by placing a serving platter over the pan and quickly inverting. The cake will slide out easily.

Slice and serve with a good quality tea.

COMRADE II CAKES

12 servings

There is no place more beautiful in the world than the coastal area of northern British Columbia, and no place from which to experience it more fully than a boat. I am blessed with a dear friend of many years' standing, Eric Hunter, who always gives a warm welcome whenever I visit him during the summers he serves as a federal Fisheries Patrol officer.

In such a circumstance, however, I am torn between wishing to do my share of the work and losing myself in the enchantment of those effulgent waters. These cakes are a resolution of that conflict. There are no elaborate cooking tools; no fragile operations to be ruined by a pitch or roll; no soaking/waiting times. A pleasing aroma wafts from the galley to the skipper concentrating at the wheel. A few minutes to assemble the ingredients; then it's elbows on the sterndeck while the cakes metamorphose in the diesel-fired stove. Do eat these with a decent cup of tea in your own place of reverie. . . .

435 mL	flour	1¾ cups
60 mL	dried coconut	¼ cup
185 mL	sugar	¾ cup
250 mL	butter, softened	1 cup
1	egg	1
60 mL	fresh, peeled and finely grated ginger, loosely packed	¼ cup

Pre-heat oven to 175°C (350°F).

In a medium bowl mix all ingredients together using fingers. Transfer to a square 2L (2qt) pan. Smooth the top with the back of a metal spoon. Place in oven for 40 minutes.

Immediately upon removal, mark off portions with the spine of a kitchen knife so cake will cut easily. (Use an up/down chopping motion to prevent "crumb-drag.")

Allow to cool fully, slice and eat at your leisure.

Variation: Omit the ginger; increase sugar to 250 mL (1 cup), and add 5 mL (1 tsp) vanilla or almond extract.

MANDALAY

By the old Moulmein Pagoda, lookin' eastward to
the sea,
There's a Burma girl a-settin', and I know she
thinks o' me;
For the wind is in the palm trees, and the temple
bells they say:
"Come you back, you British soldier; come you
back to Mandalay!"

RUDYARD KIPLING (1865–1936)
MANDALAY

GINGER SWEET MORSELS

12 servings

Not cake, candy or cookie, these sweet, gingery edibles are delicious at coffee break.

3	eggs	3
125 mL	sugar	½ cup
15 mL	flour	1 tbsp
125 mL	butter, softened	½ cup
30 mL	ginger marmalade	2 tbsp
8 mL	ground ginger	½ tbsp
250 mL	milk	1 cup
125 mL	dried coconut	½ cup

Pre-heat oven to 190°C (375°F).

In a medium bowl beat the eggs. Add remaining ingredients in order listed, blending after each addition.

Pour mixture into greased loaf pan. Bake for 1–1¼ hours. Remove from oven. With the blunt side of a kitchen knife, mark out 12 blocks.

Allow to cool at room temperature for 1–2 hours. Refrigerate for 4–6 hours. Cut along lines. Remove fudgey squares from pan and *invert* onto plate.

Serve.

LIME FROTH

5–6 servings

This light, airy dessert needs a minimum of 1 hour in the refrigerator before serving. You will need an electric mixer as well as a wire whisk.

4	eggs, separated	4
1	zest of a lime, very finely grated	1
60 mL	fresh lime juice	¼ cup
45 mL	water	3 tbsp
185 mL	sugar	¾ cup
3 mL	vanilla	½ tsp
250 mL	grated fresh or frozen coconut	1 cup

With a wire whisk beat egg yolks in top of a double boiler. Gradually add lime zest, juice, water and 125 mL (½ cup) of the sugar, whisking constantly. (It takes at least 10 minutes for the custard to thicken.) Remove from hot water and set aside.

In a separate, medium mixing-bowl, and using an electric mixer, beat the egg whites until stiff. Add the vanilla and remaining 60 mL (¼ cup) sugar slowly, beating continuously until the meringue is glossy.

Switch back to the wire whisk as your mixing tool, and fold-in half of the warm yolk-custard, followed by the coconut, and finally the remaining custard. Blend gently and well. Pour into serving bowls (coconut half-shells?) and refrigerate.

POST-PARTY BISCUITS

10 servings

Post-party biscuits are a means of using the left-over cream of coconut mixer used for making piña coladas and other exotics. The label on the can will usually list sugar, salt, flavorings, bindings, and preservatives in the ingredients, so it is not to be confused with simple coconut cream (the first and/or double top-skim of coconut milk which has been allowed to set). By the way, this is the sole-exception item of this book: all other recipes use unsweetened coconut products.

| 212 g | roll commercial biscuit dough | 7½ oz |
| | Left-over portion of cream of coconut mixer | |

Pre-heat oven to 190°C (375°F).

With your thumb make a depression in the center of each biscuit, and pull up the outer edges slightly to make a set of mini dough-bowls. Drop a 3 mL (½ tsp) blob of cream of coconut into each depression.

Place the biscuits on an ungreased cookie sheet and bake for approximately 12 minutes or until golden brown. Serve hot.

SEMOLINA QUICK DESSERT

4–5 servings

Semolina is a milled product of durum wheat and therefore qualifies as a pasta. Since it is usually cooked only to serve in a grain capacity, it tends to be overlooked as the useful staple it really is. It contains mostly endosperm particles which get soft and mushy if overcooked. This quality makes quite desirable desserts.

375 mL	semolina	1½ cups
1 mL	sea salt	¼ tsp
60 mL	raisins	¼ cup
398 mL	coconut milk	14 oz
250 mL	water	1 cup
8 mL	vanilla	½ tbsp
125 mL	date sugar (or corn syrup)	½ cup

Place the first five ingredients in a medium saucepan. Bring to the boil. Reduce to very low heat, stir and cook gently for 12 minutes, stirring occasionally.

Add the vanilla and date sugar. Cook another 2 minutes stirring constantly.

Serve hot or cold, with or without apricot jam.

Variation: Top each serving with a scoop of coffee ice cream.

SOUR CHERRY PUDDING

9–10 servings

Married to roast moose, pork or wild fowl, this recipe whispers of the divine ambrosia of our forefathers.

Served warm or cold with sour cream or evaporated milk, it also makes a luscious dessert.

796 mL	jar red, sour, pitted cherries in light syrup	28 liquid oz
150 g	KTC creamed coconut, grated*	5¼ oz
30 mL	cornstarch	2 tbsp
45 mL	corn syrup	3 tbsp
8 mL	vanilla	½ tbsp

Pour syrup from cherries into a medium saucepan.

Grate block of creamed coconut into the syrup. Add cornstarch. Stir over medium heat until there are no lumps.

Lightly mash the pitted cherries with a fork. Add to the saucepan. Add the vanilla.

Bring to a slow boil. Simmer, stirring, for 6–8 minutes. Transfer to serving bowl.

Serve warm or refrigerate overnight and serve cold.

Variation: As a meat accompaniment, substitute dried fruits such as prunes, apricots or figs for the cherries.

Plump 225 g (8 oz) prunes for 4 hours in 3 cartons (750 mL or 25 fl.oz) coconut water. Proceed as above.

*See *Supply Sources* at the back of this book.

STEAMED PUDDING WITH CRANBERRY SAUCE

6 servings

The type of steamer you have will dictate the size of mold(s) you will use for this dessert. I use a Chinese bamboo steamer on top of a large saucepan, with a metal pie-plate for the pudding, and these directions are written accordingly. Do adapt to your own equipment, as the recipe is quite forgiving.

You may wish to double the quantity of tangy sauce to top other dishes. (It is wonderful on coffee-flavored ice cream.)

FOR THE PUDDING:

3	eggs	3
125 mL	sugar	½ cup
1 mL	salt	¼ tsp
3 mL	almond extract	½ tsp
23 mL	coconut oil, softened if solid	1½ tbsp
185 mL	fresh or frozen grated coconut	¾ cup
250 mL	flour	1 cup

FOR THE SAUCE:

375 mL	frozen, unsweetened cranberries	1½ cups
110 mL	corn syrup	½ cup - 1 tbsp
4 mL	coconut extract	¾ tsp
10 mL	lime juice	2 tsp

Optional topping: sour cream

To make the pudding:

Grease the pie-pan or other utensil you will be using to hold the pudding.

Using a wire whisk, cream the eggs and sugar in a medium bowl.

Switch to a wooden spoon, and one-by-one add the remaining ingredients in sequence, stirring after each addition. Ensure that the flour is especially well blended.

Pour mixture into pie plate or pudding bowl.

Steam for 40 minutes. Slice into 6 wedges. Keep warm.

To make the sauce:

Place all ingredients in a blender and purée.

Serve the pudding very warm with the topping very cold. Sour cream is also a delicious complement.

During the seventeenth century the Port of London, England, designated commercial coconuts as *coker-nuts* to avoid confusion with cocoa. To this day, in popular parlance around the docks, one still hears "cokers." The word has long-standing association with the Old Dutch *kokernoot*.

TAPIOCA PUDDING

8–10 servings

If having to cook for someone whose diet needs to be both wheat-free and dairy-free, this recipe is an everyday winner. Tapioca is made from the nutritious root-starch of cassava, also called manioc. Tapioca is available in either small (sometimes called "seed") or large pearls. Emotions tend to run extraordinarily high regarding preference. The pudding is a staple dessert in British schools. In mine it was referred to as frog spawn, and I now therefore insist on using the small variety to distance myself from the concept. A friend tells me that in her school they called it slugs eyes, and she therefore insists on using only the large. (Recipe portions are interchangeable but both the soaking and cooking times need to be tripled.) In spite of the negative appellations, tapioca pudding is a universally popular dish with children. For this reason I have created the recipe to make a large batch. Quantities may be halved to suit.

250 mL	small seed tapioca	1 cup
375 mL	water	1½ cups
1 L	coconut milk	4 cups
3 mL	sea salt	½ tsp
4	eggs, separated	4
	finely grated zest of	
	1 lemon	
250 mL	granulated sugar	1 cup

In a large saucepan soak tapioca in the water for 1 hour.

Add coconut milk, sea salt, lightly beaten egg yolks, and lemon zest. Bring to boil over medium heat, stirring constantly.

Reduce to very low heat and simmer uncovered for 15 minutes, stirring often.

Beat eggs whites with sugar until soft peaks form. Fold a cup of the hot tapioca into the egg whites, then gently fold mixture back into saucepan. With a wire whisk, stir over low heat for 3–5 minutes.

Serve warm or cold, with or without stewed fruit.

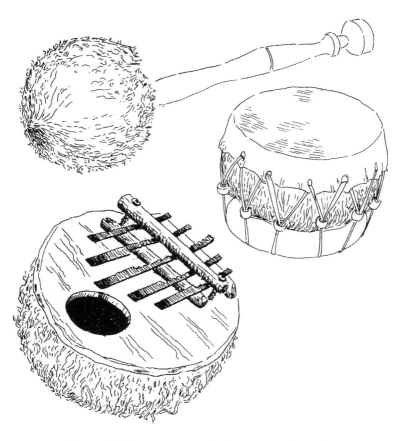

Toy musical instruments made from coconuts by author.

UBE CAKE WITH SOUR CREAM TOPPING

2 cakes yielding 12/16 servings each

Ube is a variety of yam from the Philippines. When powdered for use as a flour, it imparts a rich mauve color to food and also lends a hint of light fruitiness. I cannot explain why men in particular like this confection. It freezes well and can be your trump card at time of need.

FOR THE CAKE:

454 mL	butter, softened	1 lb
750 mL	sugar	3 cups
6	eggs	6
114g	package powdered ube*	4 oz
875 mL	flour	3½ cups
15 mL	baking powder	1 tbsp
250 mL	buttermilk	1 cup
5 mL	coconut extract	1 tsp
5 mL	almond extract	1 tsp

Preheat oven to 175°C (350°F). Grease and flour 2 square 20 x 20 cm (8" x 8") pans.

In a large bowl cream the butter and sugar. Add eggs singly, beating after each addition. Set aside. Gradually add and mix the remaining ingredients, alternating additions of the flour and buttermilk.

Pour the mixture equally into the prepared pans and bake for 50 minutes or until an inserted knife blade comes out clean. Allow to cool at room temperature for half an hour. Run the blunt edge of a knife around the sides of the cakes before inverting on plates.

*See *Supply Sources* at the back of this book.

FOR THE TOPPING:

500 mL	low-fat sour cream	2 cups
5 mL	almond extract	1 tsp
1250 mL	fresh or frozen shredded coconut	5 cups
250 mL	powdered (confectioner's) sugar	1 cup

In a medium bowl blend all ingredients thoroughly. With a spatula, spread lavishly on the tops of the cakes.

Ube cake has such charming visual appeal that I suggest you bring it to the table sliced. A sprinkle of edible flowers on the serving platter raises the whole event to festive standards. Some edible flowers are pansies, nasturtiums and dahlias.

The captioned question of the day on page 1 of the Friday, May 6, 1932 issue of the *Honolulu Star-Bulletin* was "Do Coconuts Ever Really Fall On Anybody's Head"? The text read:

Although some people have expressed fear of coconuts falling on their heads, nobody as yet has submitted proof, according to Clarke Irvine, who is endeavoring to secure evidence.

While ripe nuts often drop near persons standing under palms or passing directly beneath them, "a miss is as good as a mile" is evidence, South Sea travelers say, that the cocopalm never hits anybody.

Mr. Irvine has a letter from the mainland asking for data on the subject, and so he has sent out a query to various travelers and authorities requesting information.

Anyone having any record of accidents due to a coconut falling on anybody, is requested to write to Mr. Irvine at 413 Hawaiian Electric building.

"During my travels in Fiji, Samoa, tropical Australia, Borneo and the Philippines, where the coconut is raised commercially for copra and coir—the husk fiber—I have never heard of one instance of a nut falling on anybody," Mr. Irvine says, "and I have yet to meet the first person who has ever heard of this sort of an accident."

The ensuing years yielded negligible data until another page 1 article appeared in the *Honolulu Star-Bulletin* of March 23, 1950:

Coconut Shower Basis of $15,000 Suit
John Carreiro Seeks Damages;
Cluster of 34 Hit Him in Head

Falling coconuts have conked only four persons in 15 years, records indicate—but the most recent victim of this tropical trouble seeks $15,000 in damages from the city.

* * *

The victim is John Carreiro, 77, of 2391 Koa Ave., who was felled by the coconut shower last September 23.

* * *

He had been standing in the shade of a coconut tree along Aukai St. when the cluster and attached branch, tumbled from overhead.

His attorney, James A. Leavey, in a letter to city fathers today, points out the offending tree was outside the private property on Aukai St.

Hence it is city property.

He points out Mr. Carreiro was taken to Queen's hospital after the freak accident where he remained confined for 2½ months.

The victim "has suffered and is still suffering severe pain and inconvenience as a result of his injuries and is permanently disabled," the attorney's letter states.

* * *

September newspaper accounts of the accident report the injured man was treated for concussion, possible spine injury and abrasions about the head and face.

The attorney's letter says Mr. Carreiro has paid out $1,000 in hospital and doctor bills.

The $15,000 in damages is asked for the city's "failure to fulfill its obligations as a government agency."

This apparently is intended to indicate failure to trim the coconut tree properly.

DRINKS, CONFECTIONS & ICE CREAMS

6

The following 5 recipes for sherbet, ice-mold, and ice creams can be made in virtually every kitchen. Numbers 1 and 2 require a freezer section in the refrigerator plus an ice-cube tray (#1) and a Bundt pan or other metal mold (#2). Numbers 3 and 4 are designed for a hand-cranked ½-1L (1 pt-1 qt) unit with an inner, gel-filled metal canister. Number 5 employs the traditional, made-in-a-bucket, rock salt and crushed ice model, manual or electric.

#1: SOUR-SOP SHERBET

4 servings as dessert or
6 servings as between-courses refresher

The coconut cream and water may be replaced by 500 mL (2 cups) coconut milk enriched with extra coconut milk powder. (Follow suggestions on package.)

250 mL	coconut cream	1 cup
250 mL	water	1 cup
375 mL	confectioner's (powdered) sugar	1½ cups
15 mL	vanilla	1 tbsp
3 60g (180g)	sachets sour-sop pulp*	3 2oz (6oz)

Whisk all ingredients together. Remove divider from ice cube tray and pour in mixture. You may need 2 trays. Freeze.

Garnish with a few cherries or berries but do not add too many for they will overpower the delightful sour-sop flavor.

Sour-sop (guanabana) is a large, slightly acidic, pulpy fruit from the West Indies. It makes refreshing desserts and drinks which are particularly soothing on summer days. See Supply Sources *at the back of this book.*

#2: ICE-MOLD WITH TOASTED FLAKES

5–6 servings

A bundt pan gives this ice-mold an attractive appearance. However, a regular ring-mold or stainless-steel mixing bowl are equally functional.

500 mL	whipping cream	2 cups
300 mL	can sweetened condensed milk	10 oz
250 mL	water	1 cup
15 mL	vanilla	1 tbsp
500 mL	toasted coconut flakes (see p. 89)	2 cups

In a large freezer-safe bowl, whip the cream until stiff. Set aside.

In a small bowl, whisk the condensed milk, water and vanilla extract together. Fold mixture into the whipped cream. Freeze until mushy. Remove from freezer and stir in toasted flakes.

Transfer to bundt pan. Freeze until solid.

When ready to serve, invert pan over serving platter. Place a hot, wet tea towel over the pan. The ice-mold will slither out easily.

Serve immediately.

#3: RUM-FLAVORED COCONUT ICE CREAM

Yields approximately 1L (1 qt).
Halve the ingredients to make 500 mL (1 pt).

Salmonella bacteria have grown bigger and better in recent years, so one needs to be confident of the source of the eggs called for in this recipe. Current practice is to omit uncooked eggs from culinary fare. However, I have faith that before long the problem will be overcome, and this recipe will endure. At present, salmonella has not been a problem in Canada, but my vanity is that this recipe will travel beyond Canada's shores.

I make this easy ice cream regularly, and everyone always enjoys it. As home-made ice creams generally do not contain stabilizers or emulsifiers, it is best to eat them within a couple of hours after freezing. An electric mixer produces the best results, but hand mixing will do.

2	eggs	2
185 mL	sugar	¾ cup
354 mL	can evaporated milk	12 liquid oz
500 mL	cream	2 cups
10 mL	rum extract	2 tsp
125 mL	fresh or frozen shredded coconut	½ cup

Beat eggs with the sugar until mix thickens. Add remaining ingredients. Mix well. Transfer to the frozen unit of your ice cream maker and follow manufacturer's directions.

The ice cream will be ready to eat in about 20 minutes, or you may remove the stirrer and place the container in the freezer for a couple of hours.

#4: COFFEE ICE CREAM

Makes 500 mL (1pt)

In professional kitchens, this quantity is supposed to be sufficient for 4 persons, but in my family of voracious eaters one batch is regarded as an individual portion!

3	egg yolks	3
90 mL	sugar	6 tbsp
125 mL	coconut milk	½ cup
250 mL	whipping cream	1 cup
60 mL	coffee beans	¼ cup
3 mL	vanilla (optional)	½ tsp

In a large bowl whisk the egg yolks and sugar together until mix thickens. Set aside.

Rinse a saucepan. Leave the inside wet. Combine the coconut milk, whipping cream and coffee beans in the saucepan. Scald (do not bring to boil). Leave to steep for 1 hour. Pour half this mix into yolks/sugar mixture. Stir. Add remainder. Stir again.

Wash the saucepan and pour the custard in it. Add the vanilla (optional). Cook over medium heat, stirring, until custard thickens. Remove from heat. Strain into a clean bowl. Cover and cool at room temperature.

When cool, transfer to the frozen unit of your ice cream maker and follow manufacturer's directions.

Serve with chocolate wafers.

#5: PEA SOUP ICE CREAM

makes 1 L (1 qt)

In the Occidental mind, legumes are not usually associated with desserts. If you have ever enjoyed black-bean shave-ice in Hawaii or Chinese red-bean sweet-rolls in Canada, split-pea ice cream is but another gentle variation on this Oriental theme.

After eating delectable pea-and-coconut popsicles on East Powell Street in Vancouver, BC, I developed the following recipe with Western tastes in mind. It is created for the traditional rock salt and crushed ice type of ice cream machine.

Yellow-pea soup is the tastier choice for this recipe. However, use the green variety if that is all that is available. (In either case, make sure it is without bits of ham floating in it)!

Suggestion: If your diners have strong, preconceived notions about the "shoulds and oughts" of desserts, you initially may choose to serve this as a "savory snack." (I offered this to an elderly gentleman who heard "pea soup" as "peaches." He kept returning for more—until he heard The Truth!)

6	egg yolks	6
185 mL	sugar	¾ cup
3 mL	ground ginger	½ tsp
250 mL	whipping cream	1 cup
319 g	can condensed yellow-pea soup	11¼ oz
250 mL	coconut milk	1 cup
147 mL	can evaporated milk	5 liquid oz

In a large bowl whisk the egg yolks, sugar and ground ginger together until mix thickens. Set aside.

In a wide saucepan, combine the whipping cream, pea soup, coconut milk and evaporated milk. Bring to just below the boil, stirring constantly to prevent burning. Remove from heat. Pour half of this into the egg/sugar bowl. Stir. Add the remainder. Stir until well blended.

Transfer to a clean saucepan. Cook over medium heat, stirring, until the custard thickens (10–15 minutes). Remove from heat. Cover and allow to cool before placing in ice cream maker for freezing.

Serve with ginger snaps.

A SUMMER'S DAY PICK-ME-UP DRINK

1 serving

I doubt this healthful beverage could be sold commercially as the quantity of vitamin C is approximately 500 mg and far exceeds the recommended daily allowance (60 mg). Ironically, many commercial soft drinks contain 25–35 mL (5–7 tsp) sugar, and I fervently wish it were illegal to sell these drinks to children.

250 mL	fresh or cartoned coconut water	1 cup
1	lime wedge	1
.63 mL	powdered (crystallized) vitamin C	⅛ tsp

To the coconut water add the juice of the lime wedge and the vitamin C powder. Whisk together.

Put up your feet, sip slowly and be refreshed!

CRYSTALS OF VEGETABLES

1 serving

*If you play sports or have sought holistic health coun-
selling, you probably have been introduced to crystals
derived from such vegetables and grains as carrots, broccoli, cabbage, cauliflower, and young barley. There are also combinations
available which have names with a "phyto" prefix. One is instructed to
mix 5–15 mL (1 tsp - 1 tbsp) crystals in 125–250 mL (½–1 cup) water.
This recipe gives an extra kick due to the potassium and enzymes in
coconut water. Create your own refreshment delights by experimenting
with other types of crystals.*

| 250 mL | individual carton coconut water | 1 cup |
| 23 mL | carrot crystals | 1½ tbsp |

Stir ingredients together in a glass and drink.

ICE CUBES

To perk cordials on hot summer days, put coconut water in your ice
cube trays. A few borage flowers embedded within the cubes are to
be especially favored with iced mint tea.

FUDGE BALLS

25 servings

400 g	dried coconut, fine shred	14 oz
125 mL	sweetened condensed milk	½ cup
3	egg yolks	3
15 mL	vanilla	1 tbsp
30 mL	coconut oil or softened butter	3 tbsp
125 mL	granulated sugar	½ cup
45 mL	cocoa powder	3 tbsp

In a medium saucepan, mix the coconut, condensed milk, vanilla and egg yolks. On medium heat and stirring frequently, cook until thickened, about 15 minutes. Remove from heat.

When mixture is cool enough to handle, mold firm balls of the fudge by rolling between your greased palms. They should be slightly smaller than a golfball. Roll all the fudge balls in the sugar. For color and taste contrast, roll only half of them in the cocoa powder. Arrange on a serving platter. Cover lightly with waxed paper and refrigerate for 1–2 hours.

Serve chilled.

HAUPIA

25 servings

There are several theories concerning the origin of the coconut. For reasons of the striking similarities in coconut language, as well as logical routing, I favor the argument for Old World genesis, with India and Malaysia topping the likely candidates' list. The name for this recipe illustrates my point. Haupia is Hawaiian for this rich sweetmeat. (I have not called it "dessert," as we of the West think of this as a full course. Haupia's function seems to be more along the line of an after-dinner mint.) From India there is a similar confection called Hawpe. Gelling agents vary from cornstarch, rice starch, gelatin to agar agar.

125 mL	cornstarch	½ cup
125 mL	water	½ cup
375 mL	coconut milk	1½ cups
75 mL	sugar	5 tbsp
5 mL	vanilla	1 tsp

In a medium jug, dissolve the cornstarch in the water. Set aside.

In a medium saucepan over medium heat, bring the coconut milk and sugar to a boil, stirring frequently. Slowly add the cornstarch mixture to the saucepan on the boil, stirring continually. Add the vanilla. Keep stirring until the mixture comes to the boil again and all lumps are removed. Pour into a 20 x 20 cm (8" x 8") pan. Allow to set firmly in the refrigerator for several hours, preferably overnight.

With a hot, wet knife, cut into 25 squares. Serve.

Variation: If you wish to serve this in a pretty shape, grease the mold with a little coconut oil before filling. To remove, release the edges with the back of a kitchen knife. Invert mold onto serving platter. The haupia will slither out easily. Cut into squares with a hot, wet knife. Add a few edible flowers for garnish.

HOT CHOCOLATE

1 serving

This non-dairy drink may be made with fresh, canned or reconstituted powdered coconut milk.

250 mL	coconut milk	1 cup
8 mL	pure low-fat cocoa powder	½ tbsp
	sweetener to taste (optional)	

Place coconut milk in a large mug. Add the cocoa powder (and optional sweetener). Whisk. Microwave for 1–2 minutes.

IRISH MOSS SHAKE

6 servings

Savi, co-owner of the "Caribbean and Newfoundland Market" (see Supply Sources *at the back of this book), told me that the Caribbean people make a very popular shake from Irish Moss. She wrote me a list of the ingredients but neither the quantities nor the method. She is therefore absolved of all responsibility for the recipe below. I have no idea whether or not it approximates the traditional, but I suspect that it does not. I wanted Savi to sample my testings, but at the time of going to print she was on an extended visit with her family in Trinidad. For the record, I did have a lot fun playing with this. . . .*

The straining after cooking is essential, as there will be little pieces of sea shell in the drink. They are nigh-to-impossible to pick out beforehand.

27 g	packet dried Irish Moss	.06 lb (.95 oz)
1½ L	water	6 cups
23 mL	flax seed powder	1½ tbsp
30 mL	vanilla	2 tbsp
125 mL	powdered coconut milk	½ cup
196 g	can sweetened condensed milk	14 oz

In a medium saucepan, bring the Irish Moss and water to a boil. Reduce heat. Simmer, stirring occasionally, until the strands have disintegrated and the moss is well blended, about 15 minutes.

Strain through a fine mesh or muslin into a large pouring vessel. Add the other ingredients. Stir until smooth. Pour into glasses.

Drink while lukewarm.

Variation: If you leave this in the refrigerator for a few hours or overnight, it will settle to the consistency of a pudding which can be eaten with a spoon. Aaron's bit of wisdom: it can be returned to drink form by adding a couple of shots of rum and giving it a quick whirl in the blender.

Take your pick!

CARBON GRANULES

The carbon granules for domestic water filters are usually made from coconut shells.

JAM (KAYA)

Makes 185 mL (3/4 cup) approximately

250 mL	warm water	1 cup
60 mL	coconut milk powder	¼ cup
250 mL	granulated sugar	1 cup
3 mL	ground ginger	½ tsp

In a shallow saucepan, dissolve coconut powder in the warm water. Add the sugar and ginger. Stir, and then cook over very low heat to prevent burning. Do not continue to stir, but with a spatula scrape the drying syrup from the sides to the center of the pan.

Remove from heat when jam thickens, about 20–25 minutes. Allow to cool. Transfer to jar or serving dish.

Serve on crackers or toast.

CRAB

Birgus latro is the coconut crab, also known as 'purse crab' and 'palm crab.' Indigenous to the islands of the South Pacific, it is a terrestrial creature which feeds on coconuts.

SOUR-SOP DELIGHT

1 serving

For help with ingredients see Supply Sources *at the back of this book.*

When mixing beverages, reconstituted powdered coconut milk is always an option for fresh or canned coconut milk. Its advantage is that the consistency can be varied to complement the other ingredients.

250 mL	coconut milk	1 cup
60–120 g	sour-sop pulp	2–4 oz
	(1 or 2 sachets)	

Whisk together in large glass. Sweeten to taste. Serve.

Variation: Sour-sop is also available in cans as a ready-mixed drink. It is usually labeled "Sour-sop Nectar" and contains water, a sweetening agent, plus a stabilizer. Use this product in a 1:1 ratio with coconut milk. It is a more costly way to make the drink. Perhaps it is also less attractive because the amount of sugar is not under consumer control.

NOTICE OFTEN SEEN ON LONDON, U.K.,
FRUIT VENDORS' BARROWS

No pincha da peaches.
Pincha da coconuts!

SOY DRINK

1 serving

125 mL	soy milk	½ cup
125 mL	coconut milk	½ cup
15 mL	honey or corn syrup	1 tbsp

Place ingredients in a tall glass. Whisk briskly. Serve.

Variation: Substitute 30 mL (2 tbsp) chocolate or caramel sauce for the honey.

THE SECOND CANADIAN COLD CURE

6 servings

When the going gets rough, bugs are in full force, or your soul feels incurably world-weary, here is the magic potion.

1	hand-sized root of fresh ginger, peeled & sliced	1
1½ L	water	6 cups
135 mL	coconut syrup	9 tbsp

Place the ginger slices and water in a saucepan. Bring to the boil. Cover, reduce heat, and simmer for 30 minutes.

Strain the ginger tea into a teapot. Add the coconut syrup. Stir. (Keep in a Thermos for bedside use.)

Relax and imbibe until the world around you corrects itself.

TOASTED FLAKES

Owing to their versatility, toasted coconut flakes are a wonderful item to have on hand in the kitchen. They are delicious on ice creams (especially coffee-, rum- or vanilla-flavored). They enhance any fruit-salad or cereal, add texture to steamed vegetables or stir-fry, bolster a trail-mix, garnish a cheese-cake, or make an agreeable snack simply on their own.

Since the coconut is to be toasted anyway, the short-cut method of shell removal by baking can be used because the subsequent flavor is not at risk. (See pp. xiv-xv "To Open a Coconut.") I suggest you prepare more than one coconut at a time since the flakes keep well for a couple of weeks in an airtight container.

1 or more	coconut(s)	**1 or more**

Pre-heat oven to 175°C (350°F).

Pierce the "eyes" of each coconut. Drain the water to drink or reserve for later use with other recipes.

Bake for 1 hour. Remove from oven and allow to cool. Tap with hammer. Shells will fall off. Peel and discard testa ("skin").

Using either the potato-slicer side of a grater, or the slicing attachment of a food processor, slice all the meat. Arrange in a shallow pan. Bake for 15 minutes. (You may also use a microwave. Time will vary with model. You will need to turn the flakes at the mid-point: approximately 3–6 minutes total time.)

Allow to cool. Then place in an airtight container.

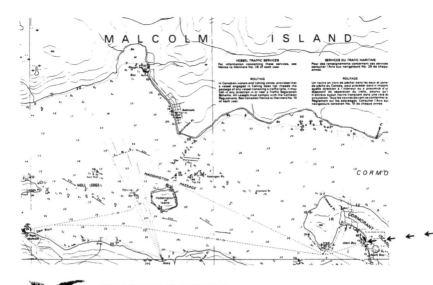

FEATURE ITEM

ABCs

24 servings

ABC is an acronym for Alert Bay Cake. This recipe is my offering to the "up island" (the northern end of Vancouver Island and its satellites) to challenge the mid-island's Nanaimo Bar. It is my dream that ABCs will become as famous and coveted as the latter, as indeed they should be.

Why the name of Alert Bay when I live in Vancouver? At some deep, intuitive level, I know Alert Bay, British Columbia, to be my mental spawning ground. Each year I gravitate to its shore with no plan, no objective, no appointment: simply an urgency to be there for a day or two. I walk alone until the moment of unity of body, mind and spirit transforms my being. Ideas (including recipes) cascade kaleidoscopically. Then, I must just as urgently leave. I am replete. That is the genesis story of ABCs as my tribute to Alert Bay.

ABCs

Use large size (not "giant") paper baking cups. Colored ones make an attractive contrast to the white topping. Bright, floral baking cups look even prettier.

This recipe can be easily halved or doubled. It may be made with fresh, canned or reconstituted powdered coconut milk. Cook the topping in a heavy-based saucepan to prevent burning.

FOR THE BASE:

250 mL	butter	1 cup
185 mL	sugar	¾ cup
125 mL	low-fat cocoa powder	½ cup
500 mL	flour	2 cups

FOR THE TOPPING:

125 mL	cornstarch	½ cup
125 mL	cool water	½ cup
625 mL	coconut milk	2½ cups
90 mL	sugar	6 tbsp
10 mL	powdered ginger	2 tsp

FOR THE GARNISH:

24	slices crystallized ginger	24

Pre-heat oven to 180°C (350°F). Line 2 1-dozen muffin pans with 24 large paper baking cups.

In a medium bowl cream the butter, sugar and cocoa powder. Add the flour and blend well.

Spoon equal amounts into the baking cups. Tamp with the back of the spoon to form a solid base on the bottom of the cups.

Bake for 25–30 minutes. Remove from oven, set aside and prepare the topping as follows:

In a small jug whisk the cornstarch with the water. Set aside.

In a heavy saucepan, stirring continuously over medium heat, slowly bring to a boil the coconut milk, sugar and powdered ginger. Give the cornstarch mixture a quick whisk to unsettle any sediment and very slowly pour into the saucepan. Stir constantly. When air bubbles start to pop, remove pan from heat and immediately spoon mixture into the baking cups. Smooth with back of spoon. Work without interruption to pour the topping into the cups, because it sets very quickly.

Garnish each cake with a crystallized ginger slice.

Allow to cool for 1 hour at room temperature and at least 1 hour in the refrigerator before serving.

Variation: Substitute 5 mL (1 tsp) vanilla for the powdered ginger, and garnish with half a glacé cherry on each cake.

BAKED APPLE
(OPTION #1)

1 serving

Granny Stannard (of my maiden name) held at-home play-readings on winter Sundays. From her local library she would borrow play-scripts for her group, and each person was assigned a part. There was no discussion about this, she being the glorious and unquestioned matriarch. She further insisted on a sound effects man, too, even when none was called for.

Entre actes, Granny would disappear into her aromatic kitchen, later emerging with a tray of hot, baked apples to be served with lashings of whipped cream. If cholesterol had been discovered, she simply ignored the fact. From such happy memories it followed naturally that in my new and beloved country of Canada I, along with dear friends, reinstated these long-nights gatherings, which came to be known as "Meetings of The Baked Apple Society."

Here follow three of the many recipes for baked apples. They are for single servings. Multiply by number of guests expected and add a few extra. Leftovers can be eaten cold a day or two later, so it is energy-efficient to bake a large batch.

1	large cooking apple, cored	1
15 mL	coconut, fresh or frozen (thawed)	1 tbsp
15 mL	orange marmalade	1 tbsp
2 mL	ground nutmeg	¼ tsp

Pre-heat oven to 150°C (300°F).

Place each apple on a square of aluminum foil large enough to envelop contents.

Using a fork, mix the remaining ingredients. Fill the center of each cored apple with the mix.

Bring sides of foil towards top and squeeze together to enclose stuffed apple.

Place in single layer on cookie sheet or pan. Bake for 1–1½ hours.

Serve hot, still foil-wrapped, with whipped cream, sour cream, non-fat yogurt, coconut cream, ice cream or English-style custard.

OPTION #2

15 mL	dried coconut	1 tbsp
8 mL	coconut butter	½ tbsp
15 mL	orange marmalade	1 tbsp
2 mL	ground nutmeg	¼ tsp

Follow directions for Option #1.

OPTION #3

5 mL	maple syrup	1 tsp
8 mL	coconut butter	½ tbsp
15 mL	dates, chopped	1 tbsp

Follow directions for Option #1.

BANANA BREAKFAST

2 servings

Here is a quick, delectable, energy–booster breakfast. Coconut milk leaves a cleaner, less cloying feel on the palate than does dairy cream.

2	bananas, sliced	2
10	dates, pitted and chopped	10
12	macadamia or cashew nuts, unsalted	12
1	large, firm, tart apple, cored and sliced	1
250 mL	coconut milk	1 cup

Optional:

15 mL	maple syrup	1 tbsp

Divide ingredients between two bowls and serve.

BIBLICAL PALMS

Palm derives from the Latin *palma,* and describes the handlike fronds of this family of tropical and subtropical trees. The literature of India and Ceylon (now Sri Lanka) references coconuts as far back as 300 B.C.

Biblical palm-waving was a symbol of triumph. To "bear the palm" was to be a winner. However, the people doubtless were using date palms as coconuts are not mentioned in this source.

BLUEBERRY CHEESE PIE

12 servings

A deep 5 cm (2") pie dish is needed for this make-a-day-ahead dream dessert. It is easy to prepare but time-consuming.

Choose blueberries which are packed in light syrup. A can will yield approximately one cup of berries, drained. If volume is slightly less, use the syrup from the can for the filling; add water to make up the required amount for the topping.

FOR THE CRUST:

185 mL	flour	1¼ cups
60 mL	confectioner's (powdered) sugar	¼ cup
125 mL	very finely chopped almonds	½ cup
125 mL	butter, softened	½ cup

FOR THE FILLING:

500 g	cream cheese	1 lb
125 mL	dried coconut, medium shred	½ cup
125 mL	sugar	½ cup
2	eggs	2
125 mL	blueberry syrup (see note above)	½ cup
3 mL	almond extract	½ tsp

FOR THE TOPPING:

60 mL	flour	¼ cup
60 mL	sugar	¼ cup
125 mL	blueberry syrup	½ cup
60 mL	water	¼ cup

| 398 mL | can blueberries, drained but keep syrup | 14 liquid oz |
| 185 mL | whipping cream | ¾ cup |

Pre-heat oven to 175°C (350°).

To make crust: In a medium bowl, mix all the crust ingredients. Press dough firmly against bottom and sides of deep pie dish. Bake for 22 minutes.

To make filling: In a medium bowl, beat cream cheese, coconut and syrup. When well-blended, add the sugar and eggs. Beat again until creamy.

Add filling to pie dish and bake for another 35–40 minutes, or until center passes the clean knife test. Remove from oven and allow to cool at room temperature for an hour or two.

To make topping: In a small saucepan, combine the flour, sugar, blueberry syrup and water. Stirring constantly, bring to a boil and cook for 2 minutes. Remove from heat and allow to cool.

In a medium bowl, whip the cream until stiff. Fold into the cooled gel in saucepan and stir very gently. Spoon onto cooled pie, spread evenly, and refrigerate overnight.

FRIED BANANAS

4 servings

Fried bananas with coconut ice cream is a popular dessert in much of South-east Asia. However, this batter wavers from the traditional.

Use commercial ice cream or make your own. *(See Chapter Six,* Drinks, Confections & Ice Creams.*)*

60 mL	flour	¼ cup
60 mL	rice flour	¼ cup
10 mL	cornstarch	2 tsp
125 mL	coconut water, fresh or cartoned	½ cup
2 mL	almond extract	¼ tsp
4	bananas, peeled & halved lengthwise	4
60 mL	olive oil	¼ cup

Optional:

45 mL	date sugar	3 tbsp

In a wide, shallow bowl, mix the flour, rice flour, cornstarch, coconut water and almond extract. Refrigerate for 30 minutes.

Heat oil in skillet. Dip bananas in batter and drop into hot oil. With a spatula, turn bananas to cook both sides until dark golden.

Optional: sprinkle with sugar.

Serve immediately with coconut ice cream.

NECTARINE MERINGUES

6 servings

With simple ingredients you can easily make this light dessert to follow a heavy meal.

3	large nectarines, halved and pitted	3
250 mL	cherries, pitted	1 cup
30 mL	coconut syrup	2 tbsp
2	egg whites	2
60 mL	granulated sugar	¼ cup

Pre-heat oven to 220°C (425°F).

Place nectarine halves hollow sides up in an oven-to-table dish.

In a small bowl, mash the cherries with the coconut syrup. Spoon the mixture into the nectarine hollows.

With an electric mixer, beat the egg whites until peaks hold their shape, and then gradually add the sugar. Continue beating until glossy. Gently spoon and smooth the meringue mix to cover the fruit mounds, taking care to keep the servings separate.

Bake for 8–10 minutes, or until the meringue tops are golden brown. Serve immediately.

Variation: In winter, when summer fruits are not readily available, substitute Bosc or Anjou pears and drained, canned cherries.

PLUM & CHERRY TRIFLE

9–11 servings

To this day, for my daughter Zoë, the expression "a trifle damp" quite definitely has non-standard meaning. For one thing, it is a celebratory term. For another, "trifle" is always a noun depicting a food item, and the adverb has become an adjective indicating "sodden with sherry."

This recipe is not called English Trifle *for several reasons, the first being that—oh, grievous error—it lacks jam! Secondly, most trifle recipes call for ½–1 cup sherry. This one goes overboard with 1¼–1½ cups for added festivity. Thirdly, tradition demands ladyfingers, which are not as moist as sponge cake nor as rich as pound cake. Finally, the custard in this recipe is non-dairy which adds a touch of decadence for people with dairy allergies. However, I present two toppings: Option A with whipped cream, and Option B without.*

The trifle should be made and kept in the refrigerator one or two days ahead of time, adding the topping a couple of hours before use. A glass bowl shows the pretty colors, but any large bowl will do.

304 g	pound cake, cut into 3 cm (1") cubes	10.75 oz
850 g	can purple plums, drained, pitted & lightly mashed	30 oz
850 g	can pitted cherries, drained	30 oz
310 mL	sherry	1¼ cups
60 mL	sugar	¼ cup
30 mL	cornstarch	2 tbsp
3	egg yolks	3
685 mL	coconut milk	2¾ cups
5 mL	almond extract	1 tsp

FOR THE TOPPING:

Option A — traditional

500 mL	heavy cream, whipped	2 cups
30 mL	slivered almonds, toasted	2 tbsp
30 mL	dark, bitter chocolate shavings	2 tbsp

Option B — non-dairy

60 mL	pine nuts, toasted	¼ cup
60 mL	frozen raspberries	¼ cup

If convenient, allow the cubed cake to sit on the counter overnight to dry.

Arrange half the cake cubes in the bottom of a large bowl. Cover evenly with the plums. Make another layer of cubes, and cover with the cherries.

Pour the sherry evenly all over. Set aside.

In a medium saucepan place the sugar, cornstarch, egg yolks and one cup of the coconut milk. Whisk over medium heat. Slowly add the remaining coconut milk, whisking all the time until the custard thickens. (This may seem to be an endless and unpromising task, but it metamorphoses quite suddenly, so stay with it to attain the fruits of your labor.)

Remove from heat and put aside to cool until semi-set. When cooled, spoon the custard onto the trifle, spreading evenly. Cover with clear plastic. Place in refrigerator until an hour or two before needed. Add topping before serving.

For topping, Option A: Whip the cream until it stands in stiff peaks. Spoon into a decorative ring around the edge of the trifle. Toast the almonds in a microwave for 2–3 minutes. Stir, and repeat until they are a dark, golden color. Sprinkle the toasted almonds in the center of the cream ring. Shave a chunk of chocolate on the large aperture of a grater. Sprinkle decoratively amongst the almonds.

For topping, Option B: Sprinkle the toasted pine nuts (prepared as for slivered almonds in Option A above). Arrange frozen raspberries decoratively. They will be ready to eat by serving time.

Place garnished trifle on table to admire, serve, and celebrate.

QUICKIE PEARS

2 servings

This dessert is so quick you can prepare it in the microwave while the coffee is brewing. It also makes a pleasant snack should a friend stop by.

2	firm, slightly underripe pears	2
30 mL	coconut syrup	2 tbsp

Twist off stems, and with a paring knife peel two vertical strips 1 cm wide from each pear. (This prevents bursting and also looks nice.) Slice off the bottom of each pear so that it will stand up in its own serving dish.

Place 2 pears in 2 dishes and microwave on high for 3 minutes. Remove and drizzle a tablespoon of syrup on each pear. Return to oven and cook on high for 1 minute more.

Serve alone or with a small amount of plain yogurt.

STEWED RHUBARB

5–6 servings

Many fruits can be cooked in fresh or UHT-processed coconut water to enhance their nutritional value. Coconut water is rich in potassium, has several other minerals, amino acids and enzymes. Its growth and healing properties are abundantly evident but not yet fully researched.

Try this stewed fruit (actually a vegetable which is usually used as a fruit) plain or topped with coconut milk, which is easier to digest than dairy toppings.

600 g	rhubarb, tops removed, and stalks cut into bite-size lengths	1½ lbs
5 mL	ground ginger	1 tsp
250 mL	date (or raw) sugar	1 cup
310 mL	fresh or UHT coconut water	1¼ cups

Place all ingredients in a medium saucepan. Bring to a boil, reduce heat immediately and simmer for 8–10 minutes, stirring occasionally with a wooden spoon.

Serve warm or cold.

WALNUT PIE

6 servings

Although the filling is made from scratch, this is a quick pie which is good as dessert, coffee-time snack or breakfast treat.

1	frozen pie crust	1
125 mL	butter	½ cup
250 mL	firmly-packed brown sugar	1 cup
5 mL	imitation rum extract	1 tsp
125 mL	frozen orange juice concentrate	½ cup
250 mL	dried coconut	1 cup
185 mL	walnuts, chopped	¾ cup

Pre-heat oven to 175°C (350°F).

Pierce the dough of the frozen pie shell several times with the tines of a fork. Set aside and allow to partially thaw for a few minutes while you prepare the filling.

In a shallow saucepan combine the butter, sugar, orange juice concentrate and rum extract. Using a wooden spatula, stir until the mixture is brought to a boil. Reduce temperature and allow to simmer undisturbed for 3–4 minutes.

Remove saucepan from heat and add coconut. Stir until well blended. Pour filling into pie crust. Sprinkle the walnuts evenly over the surface. Bake for 30 minutes. Remove from oven and allow to cool at room temperature for one hour before serving, or top with whipped cream or yogurt, plain or vanilla flavored.

Refrigerate pie if not serving immediately.

WHIZ PIE CRUST

6–8 servings

This is the easiest pie crust imaginable, and everyone loves it.

| 125 mL | butter, melted | ½ cup |
| 500 mL | dried coconut, finely grated | 2 cups |

Pre-heat oven to 150°C (300°F).

In a small bowl thoroughly finger-mix the ingredients. Transfer to ungreased pie-pan, and press firmly and evenly against bottom and sides. Bake for 30 minutes, or until crust is a dark, golden color. Allow to cool at room temperature. Fill with a light pudding such as lemon chiffon or vanilla custard.

Variation: This is very sticky, so use it as a base only—no sides.

| 60 mL | butter, melted | ¼ cup |
| 500 mL | fresh (or frozen), finely-grated coconut | 2 cups |

Press mixed ingredients into bottom of ungreased pie-pan. Smooth the surface with the back of a teaspoon. Bake for 40 minutes, or until a dark, golden color.

Allow to cool before topping with softened coffee or vanilla ice cream. Place in freezer for at least one hour before serving.

WINTER SALAD

5–6 servings

In many regions of our nation during winter, leafy salad greens look debilitated, and the fruit selection is minimal or expensive. This recipe is a relief from these seasonal culinary handicaps. It is a lively partner to heavy meats.

796 g	can grapefruit segments, drained	28 liquid oz
30 mL	olive oil	2 tbsp
2 mL	chile oil	¼ tsp
15 mL	red pepper sauce	1 tbsp
15 mL	lime juice	1 tbsp
30 mL	soy sauce	2 tbsp
8 mL	crushed garlic	½ tbsp
1	medium yellow onion, peeled & diced	1
60 mL	fresh or frozen shredded coconut	¼ cup
226 g	can avocado dip (guacamole)	8 oz

Cut grapefruit segments in bite-size pieces and place in center of salad bowl. Set aside.

In a small skillet mix and heat the olive oil, chile oil, red pepper sauce, lime juice, soy sauce and garlic. Add the onion and coconut and sauté until lightly browned, mixing well. Pour entire contents onto the mound of grapefruit.

Spoon the avocado dip in a ring around the salad.

Serve immediately.

YOU-GUESSED-IT PIE

6 servings

A simple, worthy dessert warm or cold. This pie and a top quality Darjeeling tea were born to be partners in life's course.

1	pie shell, frozen	1
2	eggs	2
500 mL	dried coconut	2 cups
8 mL	imitation maple extract	½ tbsp
30 mL	lime juice	2 tbsp
60 mL	water	¼ cup
125 mL	raw sugar (brown)	½ cup

Pre-heat oven to 175°C (350°F).

Place frozen pie shell in oven for 5 minutes. Remove. With a knife, make a few short slashes in the bottom of the crust. Set aside.

Break the eggs into a medium bowl and beat lightly with a fork. Add the remaining ingredients. Stir with wooden spoon.

Transfer mix to pie shell. Smooth surface with the back of spoon.

Bake until light brown: about 25–30 minutes.

Serve warm with vanilla ice cream, or refrigerate overnight and serve cold, without topping.

Coconut-cup mounted in silver-gilt, c. 1490. New College, Oxford

9

APPLE SOUP

4 servings

Because it arose, entire and perfect, out of a dream, I wanted to name this "R.E.M. Soup." A good friend pointed out that such an appellation would be too self-indulgent, communicating little to the harried person trying to get a meal on the table. In any case, this dish is easy to prepare and tastes like a dream!

3	cooking apples, peeled, cored and sliced	3
3	stalks of celery, strings removed and diced	3
398 mL	can cream-style corn	13½ oz
15 mL	minced garlic	1 tbsp
3 mL	ground nutmeg	½ tsp
5 mL	Dijon mustard	1 tsp
250 mL	water	1 cup
250 mL	coconut water	1 cup

Place all ingredients in a medium saucepan. Bring to boil, blending contents with a wooden spoon. Reduce heat and cover. Simmer, with an occasional stir, until apples are translucent (usually 20–30 minutes).

Can be served immediately. (If in season, garnish with a bright, edible flower, such as a pansy or dahlia.)

BARLEY-RICE COMBI

5–7 servings

In my family we have an expression which borders on the vulgar, but serves to describe food that sits comfortably in the intestinal tract, sating hunger for many hours: gut liner. Here is one of our mainstay gut liners (which we sometimes serve for breakfast).

1.9 L	water	7½ cups
5 mL	powdered dulse (or kelp)	1 tsp
5 mL	basil	1 tsp
310 mL	pearl barley	1¼ cups
60 mL	dried coconut	¼ cup
375 mL	long, whole grain rice	1½ cups
15 mL	coconut oil	1 tbsp

optional: garlic-chile flaxseed oil

In a large saucepan, bring to boil the water, dulse and basil. Add the barley, coconut and rice. Bring to boil again, stir, cover and reduce heat to simmer for 45 minutes.

Add the coconut oil, stir, replace lid, turn off heat and allow to mellow for another 5 minutes.

Serve as a side-dish or as a meal unto itself. Put a bottle of garlic-chile flaxseed oil on the table for those who want to add a vibrant note to the grains.

BEAN FLOUR DUMPLINGS

5–6 servings

These satisfying and nutritious dumplings can be dropped into a variety of stews or bisques. Try them in a meat or vegetable stew, or a fish bisque. My favorite use of them is with chicken stew. The recipe works well with many types of bean flour. For your first attempt I suggest chick pea (garbanzo) or, for the more exotic, azuki. These dumplings add a gentle, interesting piquancy which does not overwhelm other ingredients in the stew.

PASTE FOR THE DUMPLINGS:

1	large chile, seeded and cut into chunks	1
5 mL	chopped garlic	1 tsp
5 mL	ground ginger	1 tsp
5 mL	ground cumin	1 tsp

Place all the above ingredients in a blender and chop coarsely. Set aside.

DUMPLINGS:

375 mL	fresh or frozen flaked coconut	1½ cups
435 mL	bean flour (see comment above)	1¾ cups
185 mL	flour	¾ cup
45 mL	olive oil	3 tbsp
30 mL	butter, melted	2 tbsp
5 mL	ground turmeric	1 tsp
3 mL	lemon pepper	½ tsp
5 mL	cayenne pepper sauce	1 tsp

With a wooden spoon and fingers, mix all the above dumpling ingredients together in a medium size bowl. Add the prepared paste. Continue mixing until evenly blended to a somewhat heavy dough. (Add a little water if needed.)

Form into golf balls by rolling between the palms of the hands. There will be about 16–18. The dumplings need to simmer for 35–45 minutes, so add them to the stew of your choice at the appropriate stage in your meal preparation.

CHICK PEA PIE

4–5 servings

For this recipe you will need a metal pan of at least 23 cm (9") diameter. It can be a loaf, pie, or any other shape pan. If a loaf pan, choose the longer cooking time.

30 mL	olive oil	2 tbsp
1	large white onion, diced	1
3	cloves garlic, peeled and finely minced	3
8 mL	dill weed	½ tbsp
8 mL	oregano	½ tbsp
1–3 mL	black pepper	¼–½ tsp
1	juice of a lime	1
3	eggs	3
1 mL	sea salt	¼ tsp
250 mL	water	1 cup
60 mL	coconut milk powder	¼ cup
125 mL	flour	½ cup
3 mL	baking powder	½ tsp
250 mL	shredded Monterey Jack cheese	1 cup
30 mL	Parmesan cheese	2 tbsp
540 mL	can chick peas (garbanzos)	19 liquid oz

Pre-heat oven to 220°C (425°F). Grease metal pan.

In a medium skillet, sauté the onion, garlic, dill, oregano, and black pepper in the olive oil for 4–5 minutes or until onion is translucent. Remove from heat. Sprinkle the lime juice over the sauté. Set aside.

In a large bowl and using a wire whisk, beat the eggs, salt, water, and coconut milk powder. Whisk in the flour and baking powder.

Gently stir in the cheeses, chick peas, and contents of the skillet. Transfer to greased pan. Bake for 30–40 minutes until surface is crusty.

Serve immediately with a good mango or other chutney. A tomato or spinach salad makes this a complete and delectable meal.

HAIR CONDITIONER

A beautician friend gave me marvellous advice for conditioning dry, brittle hair. For effectiveness it is at par, if not surpassing, a $30 salon treatment.

Purchase a jar of coconut oil. If the weather is cool, the oil will have solidified. You can easily, and as often as necessary, convert it to liquid state by removing the cap and placing the jar in a microwave for 30 seconds. Saturate your hair with the oil. Cover your head with a plastic bag. Read and/or relax in an herbal bubble-bath for an hour. Remove bag and shampoo. Your hair will be grateful and gleaming.

If you follow this procedure once a fortnight for six months, you will be amazed at the lustrousness of your tresses. (The cost will be about $6 instead of $360.)

COLD AVOCADO SOUP

4–6 servings

Offer this ocean-green, palate-pleasing soup as prelude to any grilled fish or hot curry entrée. You will need a blender or food processor.

2	medium, ripe avocados, peeled, pitted & cut into chunks	2
250 mL	plain, fat-free yogurt	1 cup
250 mL	shredded coconut, fresh or frozen	1 cup
5 mL	minced garlic	1 tsp
2	medium green chiles, seeded & diced	2
3 mL	ground turmeric	½ tsp
1	juice of a lime	1
3 mL	sea salt	½ tsp
5 mL	ground coriander	1 tsp
12–15	cardamom seeds, ground after discarding husks	12–15
750 mL	water	3 cups

In the order listed, place all the ingredients except water in a blender. Add half the water. Purée. Add remaining water. Blend briefly.

Chill before serving.

All forms of coconut used in the recipes throughout this book are unsweetened.

GRAD CORN BISQUE

5–7 servings

For many years Jack deBad has been an integral part of our family. Relationships have included teacher/student; academic proctor; tour guide assistant; fellow diner; escapade partner; colleague; friend. He has been welcomed in our homes spanning three countries on two continents. When he became a Bachelor of Arts, we hosted a dinner which began with this soup. "Grad corn bisque" became a household word the origin of which only I remembered. I cannot partake of "Grad" without memories of celebration. I hope you will attain a similar state when you enjoy this soup.

2 341 mL	cans whole kernel corn (do not drain)	2 12 liquid oz
398 mL	can coconut milk	14 liquid oz
30 mL	Worcestershire sauce	2 tbsp
5 mL	ground allspice (or nutmeg)	1 tsp
250 mL	water	1 cup
60 mL	butter	¼ cup
45 mL	cornstarch or rice flour	3 tbsp
125 mL	chopped green onion	½ cup
1	red bell pepper, seeded and finely diced	1
114 mL	can roasted and peeled diced green chiles, drained	4 liquid oz
250 mL	shredded Monterey Jack cheese	1 cup

Combine first five ingredients in a blender or food processor.

In a large saucepan, melt the butter. With a wire whisk, stir in the sauce thickener and cook until lump-free. Whisk in the green onions, the corn mixture, bell pepper, chiles and cheese. Cook while whisking until the cheese is thoroughly blended and bisque is bubbly.

Serve.

JACK'S BASMATI RICE

4 servings

Should you need a dignified, elegant rice dish to serve with seafood or meat curry, Jack-the-Grad proudly offers this basmati rice recipe.

250 mL	basmati rice	1 cup
398 mL	can coconut milk	14 liquid oz
125 mL	water	½ cup

Place all ingredients in a medium saucepan and bring to a boil.

Stir with a wooden spoon to make sure that no grains are sticking to the bottom of the pan. Reduce heat; cover, and simmer for 35–40 minutes, or until all liquid is absorbed. Stir well 2–3 times during cooking. Serve.

LEEK SOUP

4–6 servings

A simple modification adds a touch of panache to otherwise standard fare. Use a wire whisk to stir this soup.

1	package leek soup mix	1
1–2 mL	allspice	¼ tsp
398 mL	can coconut milk	13½ liquid oz

Into a medium saucepan empty contents of a package of leek soup mix. Add the allspice and the coconut milk. Complete the package's liquid requirement with water. (Most instructions call for 1–1¼ L (4–4½ cups) water and/or milk.) Cook as directed.

Variation 1: Use an asparagus soup base and proceed per above.

Variation 2: Use a broccoli soup base and proceed per above.

Unsolicited Advice: Do not try a spinach soup base: it is awful!

COSMETICS

Coconut oil is used extensively in the cosmetics industry by both low-cost and exclusive lines. A few minutes in a drug store browsing the fine print of product ingredients can prove to be interesting free entertainment. In twenty minutes thus engaged I discovered shampoo, body lotion, soap, hair conditioner, sunscreen, face cream, hand lotion, bath oil, shower gel, shaving foam, skin "perfume-cream," massage oil, lipstick, make-up, make-up remover, depilatory cream, lip salve, deodorant and styling mousse as a partial listing.

PORRIDGE

1 serving

Any self-respecting non-cook can microwave this healthy, smooth, quick breakfast or night-time snack. If cooking for more than 2 persons, use the stove-top saucepan method.

15 mL	coconut milk powder	1 tbsp
250 mL	warm water	1 cup
125 mL	rolled oats	½ cup

For the Topping: maple syrup and milk/cream to taste

With a whisk, blend the coconut milk powder and water in a microwave-proof, individual serving bowl. Add the oats. Give a quick stir and zap 2–5 minutes, depending on your model. Add toppings which please you.

Serve hot.

Non-dairy Variation: Omit coconut milk powder and make porridge with water according to directions on package. Top with maple syrup and coconut milk or cream.

RELISH YOUR DAL

4–5 servings

The word "dal," a generic term for legumes, is a reminder of where to shop. The type used for this dish is split and hulled green mung beans (yellow after this process). (See Supply Sources *at the end of this book.)*

Dal will keep in the refrigerator for 4–5 days and can be re-heated in the microwave.

375 mL	dal	1½ cups
1¼ L	water	4½ cups
250 mL	coconut water, fresh or cartoned	1 cup
185 mL	shredded coconut, fresh or frozen (thawed)	¾ cup
250 mL	zucchini (or similar) green relish	1 cup

Wash the dal and place with the water in a large saucepan. Cover and leave to soak overnight.

Bring to the boil, stir, reduce heat and simmer for 30 minutes.

Add the coconut water, coconut and relish. Stir. Bring to boil again, reduce heat and simmer for another 45 minutes. It should be mushy.

Serve warm as a main dish or with baked halibut or swordfish.

It also makes a delightful breakfast: spoon some on a plate and top with two poached eggs.

SPICY CLAM CHOWDER

10–14 servings

This is a robust dish, ideal for post-sports or a work-party event. It loses nothing of its savor by being re-heated the day after.

9	rashers* bacon, cut in 1 cm (½") pieces	9
3	large potatoes, scrubbed, blemishes removed, and diced to 1 cm (½")	3
2	medium yellow onions, peeled and diced	2
250 mL	sliced mushrooms	1 cup
794 g	can diced tomatoes in their juice	28 oz
398 mL	can coconut milk	13½ oz
500 mL	water	2 cups
3 mL	lemon pepper	½ tsp
3 mL	turmeric	½ tsp
5 mL	powdered cayenne pepper	1 tsp
2	cloves garlic, peeled and finely minced	2
3 184 g	cans chopped clams, drained, & rinsed lightly	3 6½ oz

In a skillet, sauté the bacon until fat is clear. Transfer to a very large pot. Sauté the potatoes until light gold but still firm. Transfer to the large pot. Sauté the onions and mushrooms. Transfer to the large

---

*My editor changed this noun to "slices," but I furtively reinstated "rashers" at the eleventh hour—much to my delight!

pot. Add remaining ingredients to the pot. Bring to boil, reduce heat immediately, cover and simmer for 1 hour. Stir occasionally.

Serve with garlic toast or rye bagels.

Soups — Steamer Clams

See also "Dare-To-Bouillabaisse" with steamer clams or mussels, in Chapter Eleven, *Sea-Foods &/or Sea Vegetables.*

TABOULI SALAD ON FRESH SPINACH

4–5 servings

Commercially-prepared tabouli salad mix usually comes as a package of bulgar wheat and traditional Middle Eastern herbs. You simply add water, refrigerate for half-an-hour and it is ready to serve. Here we add cucumber and coconut for a pleasing variation.

170 g	package tabouli salad mix	6 oz
1	small cucumber, peeled and diced	1
60 mL	dried coconut	¼ cup
1	bunch fresh spinach, washed	1

Follow directions on package. Add the cucumber and coconut. Refrigerate for at least ½ hour. Serve on a bed of fresh spinach leaves.

WATERCRESS & TARO SOUP

5–7 servings

Of caressing mouth-feel, this soup is a winner even when made a day ahead. (If choosing this option, halt preparation just prior to blending and refrigerate overnight. When ready to use, gently re-heat and resume main recipe instructions.)

Watercress can be purchased year round in most Asian markets selling fresh produce. Regular supermarkets usually stock it during late-summer months, especially available in July.

5–700 g	taro root, peeled, & sliced	1–1½ lb
900 mL	chicken broth	3 cups
5–7	garlic cloves, peeled, & coarsely chopped	5–7
2–3	bunches watercress, cut into short lengths after removal of thick stems	2–3
5 mL	sea salt	1 tsp
25 mL	chopped ginger	1 tbsp
398 mL	coconut milk	13½ oz

In a large saucepan or Dutch oven, place the first three ingredients. Bring to a boil, stirring occasionally. Reduce heat. Cover with lid. Simmer for 20–30 minutes, or until taro slices are soft.

Add watercress, ginger, and coconut milk. Stirring, slowly bring to a boil again. Remove from heat.

Purée soup with a handheld blender. Serve.

BEEF & LIMA BEANS FRICASSEE

10

4–5 servings

Cheaper cuts of meat may be used for this same- or day-ahead economical recipe. Suggestions are chuck or cube steak. Cooking time is 2 hours.

A leafy, green side salad with a vinaigrette dressing completes the meal. If you have difficulty finding creamed coconut, see Supply Sources *at the back of this book.*

375 mL	lima beans	1½ cups
60 mL	oil	¼ cup
570 g	beef (see note above), thinly sliced	1¼ lb
1	bunch green onions, trimmed, thinly sliced	1
750 mL	water	3 cups
60 mL	oyster sauce	¼ cup
15 mL	ground ginger	1 tbsp
30 mL	Dijon mustard	2 tbsp
5 mL	mint leaves	1 tsp
56 g	creamed coconut, grated	2 oz

Cover lima beans with cold water and leave to soak at least 4 hours or preferably overnight.

Heat oil in a skillet and sauté the beef with the onions over low heat until all the pink has gone from the meat (about 10–12 minutes). Set aside.

Drain the lima beans, rinse and drain again. Transfer to a large pot or Dutch oven and add the water. Bring to a boil. Reduce heat.

Cover and simmer for 1 hour, stirring occasionally to ensure beans are not sticking to the bottom of pan.

Add the skillet's contents, followed by the sauce, ginger, mustard and mint. Replace lid and simmer for 40 minutes. Check for sticking. (Add a little more water if necessary.)

Add the creamed coconut. Using a wooden spoon, stir thoroughly to blend. Simmer gently for another 15–20 minutes.

Serve immediately, or refrigerate, covered, and re-heat in microwave the next day.

BEEF STEAK PIE

Serves 5

Many of the cheaper cuts of beef can be used for this dish. The weight called for is net, i.e., without bones, skin or fat. As a lunch, this pie is adequate by itself. For a dinner, complete the entrée with either buttered noodles or mashed potatoes, and a small, green side salad.

45 mL	oil	3 tbsp
1	large, white onion, sliced	1
150 g	mushrooms, sliced	5½ oz
2	large tomatoes, sliced	2
700 g	beef, cubed	1½ lb
8 mL	dried lemon grass	½ tbsp
3 mL	black pepper	½ tsp
305 g	can cream of asparagus soup	10 oz
½	can water	½
60 mL	coconut milk powder	¼ cup

FOR THE TOPPING:

| 250 mL | biscuit mix | 1 cup |
| 90 mL | water | 6 tbsp |

Table Condiment: Mustard

Pre-heat oven to 200°C (400°F).

Heat oil in a large skillet. Lightly sauté the onion, mushrooms and tomatoes (4–5 minutes). Transfer with a slotted spoon to a 2L (2qt) casserole. Set aside.

Using the same oil, sauté the meat cubes, sprinkled with the lemon grass and pepper, until thoroughly browned on all sides (about 15 minutes). Combine with the vegetables in casserole.

Put the condensed soup in a separate, small bowl. Half-fill the can with water and add the coconut milk powder. Whisk until all lumps are removed. Add to the condensed soup in bowl. Stir thoroughly. Pour the mixture over the casserole contents.

Bake for 55 minutes.

Meanwhile, prepare the crust by combining the biscuit mix with water. When allotted bake time has elapsed, add blobs of topping to the casserole. Bake for another 20 minutes.

Serve. Use mustard as table condiment.

LAMB CURRY

4–5 servings

If made a day ahead and kept in the refrigerator, this wholesome dish grows tastier by the overnight blending of flavors and aromas. The curry makes into festive fare if accompanied by side dishes. Cucumber raita and currant relish go especially well. Recipes for both are given in Chapter Three, Appetizers, Condiments & Savory Snacks.

Shoulder or leg butt is a good cut for lamb curry.

For the garam masala (ground mixed spices), see Supply Sources *at the back of the book, unless there is an East Indian or an Asian market in your neighborhood.*

1	large onion	1
5 mL	garlic powder	1 tsp
250 mL	fresh or frozen (thawed) finely grated coconut	1 cup
30 mL	garam masala	2 tbsp
3	large, green chiles, seeded & diced	3
8 mL	ground coriander seed	½ tbsp
60 mL	sour cream	¼ cup
60 mL	olive oil	¼ cup
1 kg	lamb (boneless), cubed	2–2¼ lb
30 mL	soy sauce	2 tbsp
500 mL	water (or vegetable stock)	2 cups
125 mL	cashew nuts, chopped & roasted	½ cup

In a large saucepan or Dutch oven with a snug-fitting lid, place the first 7 ingredients. Stir thoroughly and set aside.

In a medium skillet, heat the oil. Add the lamb cubes and brown on all sides (10–12 minutes). Transfer to saucepan.

Add soy sauce and water (or stock). Bring to a boil, stirring continually. Reduce heat. Cover with lid. Simmer for 45–60 minutes with an occasional stir.

Remove lid. Continue simmering to reduce liquid until a thick curry is formed (10–30 minutes).

Serve hot with steamed rice. Place a bowl of chopped, roasted cashews on the table to sprinkle over the curry to taste.

LAMB-STUFFED GRAPE LEAVES

Yield: 35–40

It was tempting to call these delicacies "dolmades," but I refrained because the herbs used, plus the addition of coconut, are not really in the Greek tradition, and I would be quite dismayed to be guilty of bastardizing the cuisine of a nation which has taken this art form to such exquisite heights.

Grapevine leaves are available at Greek and Italian groceries or general delicatessen.

As an appetizer, serve 1–2 per person. As entrée, serve 5–7.

To prepare this dish, you will need a large saucepan or Dutch oven with a lid as well as a plate or similar object which will fit within the cooking utensil. Its purpose is to weight the little edibles to prevent raveling during cooking.

30 mL	oil	2 tbsp
1	medium yellow onion, diced	1
500 g	lean ground lamb	1 lb
125 mL	fresh or frozen (thawed) grated coconut	½ cup
125 mL	fresh parsley, finely chopped and loosely packed	½ cup

15 mL	dried mint leaves	1 tbsp
5 mL	ground coriander	1 tsp
375 mL	cooked basmati rice	1½ cups
500 mL	jar grapevine leaves, brine discarded	1 lb
1	juice of lemon	1
varies	vegetable stock (or water with 30 mL soy sauce)	varies

FOR THE TOPPING:

Lime wedges or Celery Sauce.
(See Chapter Three, *Appetizers, Condiments & Savory Snacks*.)

Heat the oil in a large skillet and lightly sauté the onion (4–5 minutes). Add the meat. Cook until lightly browned overall (5–7 minutes). Add the coconut, parsley, mint, and coriander. Cook gently for another 3 minutes.

Remove from heat. Stir in the cooked rice.

Place a spoonful of the mixture in the middle of a grape leaf. Wrap the leaf around it, tucking the ends underneath. Set in the bottom of the saucepan. Repeat the process until all ingredients are used up. Make a second or third layer as necessary.

Squeeze the lemon juice on top. Add the stock or soy-water to just below the surface of the top layer. Cover with plate for weight. Add lid. Bring to boil. Reduce heat and simmer for about 35 minutes. (If you are using the Celery Sauce prepare it during this simmer time.)

Remove from pan with a slotted spoon and serve. Add topping(s) at the table.

MEAT LOAF

6–8 servings

450 g	lean ground beef	1 lb
2	eggs	2
1	medium onion, diced	1
1	large tomato, diced	1
28 g	packet marinade mix for meat	1 oz
125 mL	dried coconut	½ cup
1 mL	salt	¼ tsp
227 g	mushroom stems & pieces including liquid	8 oz dr.wt.
15 mL	hot chile sauce	1 tbsp
8 mL	garlic powder	½ tbsp
185 mL	rolled oats	¾ cup

Pre-heat oven to 190°C (375°F).

Mix all ingredients in a large bowl. Transfer to oiled loaf pan. Smooth surface with wooden spoon.

Bake. After ½-hour lower oven temperature to 165°C (325°F). Continue baking for another ¾–1 hr. until an inserted knife is clean upon removal. (Total oven time: 1¼–1½ hours.)

Serve warm or cold.

ONE-PAN BEEF WITH PINEAPPLE

3–4 servings

Creamed coconut can be purchased in many ethnic grocery stores. If you have difficulty locating the product, see Supply Sources *at the back of this book.*

1	medium yellow onion, peeled & diced	1
45 mL	oil	3 tbsp
600 g	lean beef, cubed	1¼ lb
1	medium green chile pepper, seeded & diced	1
250 mL	BBQ sauce	1 cup
250 mL	water	1 cup
8 mL	minced garlic (optional)	½ tbsp
498 mL	can sliced pineapple, drained	14 liquid oz
56 g	creamed coconut, grated	2 oz

In a large skillet, sauté the onions in the oil until translucent. Push to one side and add the beef. Sauté the beef until no pink remains.

Add the chile, BBQ sauce, water and garlic (optional). Stir. Cover and simmer for ½ hour.

Quarter the pineapple slices and add to skillet. Replace lid. Simmer gently for 20 minutes.

Add the coconut and stir. Simmer for 15–20 minutes.

Serve on couscous or rice.

SLOW-COOKER CHICKEN

5–6 servings

*Here is a delectable dish which allows you to go play
tennis while it is happening and brings you compliments
from contented eaters.*

*Tikka (the last ingredient listed) can be found in East Indian food shops
or grocery stores. If unavailable, substitute your own mix of ground
cumin, caraway and cardamom to equal 5 mL (1 tsp).*

1	large, white onion, peeled & sliced	1
30 mL	butter	2 tbsp
1	chicken, skinned & cut into main pieces	1
400 mL	can coconut milk	14 fl.oz
1	cucumber, peeled & diced	1
15 mL	peeled & finely-minced fresh ginger	1 tbsp
3 mL	garlic powder	½ tsp
3 mL	ground turmeric	½ tsp
5 mL	Tikka (see note above)	1 tsp

In a small skillet sauté the onions in the butter over medium heat
until golden. Transfer onions to the slow cooker and add remaining
ingredients. With a wooden spoon stir all contents to ensure spices
are evenly dispersed and solids are coated with coconut milk.

Turn on slow cooker to High. Leave for 4–5 hours.

Serve with rice.

SPICY BEEF PIE

4–5 servings

A superior quality coconut milk (see Supply Sources *at the end of this book) is desirable for making this quick and economical dish. The powdered form may be substituted* as long as all lumps are removed from the mix prior to adding other ingredients.

489 g	packet puff pastry sheets	17¼ oz
60 mL	cooking oil	¼ cup
2	medium leeks, roots & tough green leaves discarded. Remainder thinly sliced	2
500 g	lean ground beef	1 lb
2	chile peppers, seeded & minced	2
2	medium tomatoes, diced	2
60 mL	BBQ sauce	¼ cup
8 mL	ground ginger	½ tbsp
185 mL	coconut milk	¾ cup

Pre-heat oven to 200°C (400°F) or follow directions on package.

Line a deep pie dish with a sheet of room-temperature puff pastry. Make a few short slashes in the bottom. Bake for 7–8 minutes. Set aside.

Heat the oil in a large skillet and sauté the leeks for 2–3 minutes. Add the ground beef and sauté for another 8 minutes, or until meat is no longer pink.

Combine remaining ingredients in the skillet. Simmer, stirring occasionally, for 15 minutes.

Transfer to the pie dish. Cover with another sheet of puff pastry.

Press the sides together and trim overhanging edges. Make a few short slashes in the top (to vent air). Bake for 15–20 minutes, or until crust is light brown.

Serve immediately. Steamed broccoli or carrots make a good partner for this meal.

SWEET-SOUR DUCK IN WRAPS

8 servings

By preparing the duck and rice a day ahead, you can fix this meal for company even if you have been out to work (or play) all day. A barbecued duck from a Chinese food store is the perfect purchase for this recipe. Most package directions for phyllo suggest covering the remaining phyllo with a damp towel while you work with just a few sheets at a time. Phyllo dries out and becomes brittle very quickly. I suggest a step beyond damp: use a wet cloth.

For a luncheon, simply add a few slices of the season's fresh fruit to each plate. As a dinner entrée, accompany with a light salad and whole- or multi-grain rolls. A salad of spinach, mung bean sprouts and sliced mushrooms goes well with these duck wraps.

250 mL	cranberries	1 cup
250 mL	rice	1 cup
500 mL	water (or according to package instructions)	2 cups
1	duck, cooked in any manner, with skin, fat and bones removed	1
30 mL	lemon juice	2 tbsp
60 mL	oyster sauce	¼ cup

15 mL	Dijon mustard	1 tbsp
5 mL	dried mint leaves	1 tsp
60 mL	coconut milk powder	¼ cup
454 g	package phyllo	16 oz
15 mL	melted butter or coconut oil	1 tbsp

Pre-heat oven to 200°C (400°F).

Grease a large baking pan or cookie sheet.

In a large saucepan, cook the cranberries with the rice and water (time varies with variety of rice). Remove from heat.

Pull the duck meat into shreds. Add to the cranberry-rice.

In a small bowl, combine the lemon juice, oyster sauce, mustard, mint and coconut milk powder. Stir until smooth and add to the saucepan. Mix thoroughly and form large, square patties from the rice mix. (Keep in mind that you will be making 8 "wraps.")

For one wrap, place 2–3 sheets of phyllo on a clean surface. Place the rice patty at one end and roll up, tucking the ends underneath. Put onto greased baking surface. Repeat. With a knife, make a few slashes on the surface of each roll. Brush tops with melted butter. Bake for 40 minutes or until light brown.

Serve direct from oven to table.

TURKEY AFTERTHOUGHTS IN BREAD CASKETS

3 meals or 6 snacks

If you serve this meal on the second or third day after a turkey roast, you will avoid the "Not-again!" groans which invariably accompany more ordinary left-overs.

It is a good idea to prepare the "caskets" the previous evening so that they can air and crisp overnight.

1	loaf French bread	1
51 g	packet leek soup mix	1.8 oz
125 mL	coconut milk	½ cup
1–2 mL	chile oil	¼ tsp
3 mL	lemon pepper	½ tsp
3 mL	granulated garlic	½ tsp
60 mL	water	¼ cup
1	brine from canned mushrooms (below)	1
125 mL	coconut milk powder	½ cup
227 g	can mushroom stems & pieces	8 oz net dr.wt.
1	celery stalk, finely minced	1
500–625 mL	diced, cooked turkey	2–2½ cups

Pre-heat oven to 125°C (250°F).

Remove the ends from the French bread. Cut loaf in thick (4–5 cm/1½–2") slices. With a pointed paring knife, cut along each crust's inside perimeter to ½–¾ of its depth. With your fingers tamp all the loosened bread to create a firm base inside the crust walls.

Bake on an oven rack for 35–50 minutes until dried and crisp, but not burnt. (Time will vary according to freshness of bread.) Remove from oven. Allow to air in a dry place.

Empty contents of soup-mix packet into a medium saucepan. Add the coconut milk, chile oil, lemon pepper, garlic, water, brine from the can of mushrooms, and coconut milk powder. Stir over medium heat until well blended and all lumps are removed.

Add mushroom stems and pieces, celery and diced turkey. Stir gently, cooking until mixture is warm and blended.

Spoon into bread caskets.

For a meal, serve 2 per person with a spinach salad. For a snack, serve 1 per person, unaccompanied.

Turkey: For another recipe using turkey, see "Davy Jones' Locker Bird" in Chapter Eleven, *Sea-Foods &/or Sea-Vegetables.*

APRICOT & FISH SHISHKEBAB

3 servings of 2 skewers each or 2 servings of 3 skewers each.

A boneless cut of "meaty" fish such as marlin or swordfish is the best choice for a shishkebab barbecue or broil. A cucumber side-salad in a light vinaigrette dressing, or a simple parsley garnish, is all that is required to make this a well rounded entrée. A half-dozen long bamboo skewers are needed. Partial preparation can be done the day before.

12	large, dried apricots	12
2	medium potatoes	2
	oil for rack & 6 skewers	
340 g	firm fish (see note above), 3 cm (1") thick and cut into 3–4 cm (1–1½") chunks	¾ lb
28 g	packet marinade mix for meat	1 oz
60 g	cream cheese, softened	2 oz
60 mL	dried coconut	¼ cup
3	20 cm (8") square sheets of nori, each cut into 4 equal strips	3

Place apricots in a bowl and cover with water. Leave to plump overnight.

Boil potatoes with skins on until they are cooked but still firm. Drain and leave at room temperature overnight.

When ready to assemble the kebabs, immerse fish chunks for 20–30 minutes in marinade mix prepared according to package directions. Use a large bowl.

Oil barbecue rack and set 15 cm (6") above flame source. Oil bamboo skewers.

Drain apricots and set aside.

Cut potatoes into chunks slightly larger than the fish. Add to marinade.

In a small bowl and using a fork, mash the cream cheese with the coconut. Fill the apricots with the mix. Press sides together to close. Quickly dip one end of a strip of nori into the marinade and roll around a stuffed apricot. Repeat for rest of apricots.

Onto each skewer spear a potato chunk skin side first, then a fish chunk, then a wrapped apricot. Add a second set and place on plate. Repeat, spearing two sets per skewer.

When all six are ready, place on the grill and cook for 5 minutes on "low" setting. Turn and cook for 5–8 minutes, or until fish is opaque and flakes when prodded with a fork.

Serve immediately.

 All forms of coconut used in the recipes throughout this book are unsweetened.

COD FRIED IN BATTER

3–4 servings

For moist fish and crispy batter, one needs to keep the oil hot and the batter cold. Depending on the size of your skillet, you may have to fry in 2 batches. If this is the case, keep the first batch in a pre-warmed oven.

The standard companions to batter-fried fish are "chips" and cole slaw. I prefer potatoes cooked in the microwave in lieu of french fries.

125 mL	cornstarch	½ cup
125 mL	flour	½ cup
15 mL	baking powder	1 tbsp
185 mL	water	¾ cup
125 mL	fine shred coconut, fresh or frozen (thawed)	½ cup
5 mL	ground ginger	1 tsp
680 g	cod fillets, cut into 4 cm (1½") chunks	1½ lbs
125 mL	olive oil	½ cup

In a medium bowl, mix the cornstarch, flour, baking powder and water. Set aside.

Using a fork, mix the coconut and ginger in a small bowl. Add this to the batter. Refrigerate for 1 hour.

Dip the cod pieces into the batter, making sure both sides are covered.

In a large skillet, heat the oil to at least 190°C (375°F). Drop the battered cod into the hot oil and cook each side 2–3 minutes (time varies with thickness of filet). Do not overcook.

Serve immediately. (It is a good idea to seat dining-dawdlers at at the table *before* serving.)

DARE-TO-BOUILLABAISSE WITH STEAMER CLAMS OR MUSSELS

4 servings

Traditionally, bouillabaisse was made with fish-heads and scraps of all kinds of seafoods boiled together to yield a nutritious base. This broth was strained and re-heated at mealtime with fresh, edible portions of fish. These days, unless you live on a boat or near a harbor quay, it is quite difficult to get the traditional ingredients, for the reason that they are used in commercial pet food and/or fertilizer.

Here follows, for your dining pleasure, a less smelly, delectable version of bouillabaisse with two coconut products making it decidedly different. As with the traditional model, you can make the base stock ahead of time if you wish.

2 398 mL	cans clam nectar (not chowder)	2 14 liquid oz
2 250 mL	cartons coconut water	2 8 oz
284 mL	can condensed tomato soup	10 liquid oz
2	soup cansful of water	2
1	bunch parsley, stems discarded and leaves coarsely chopped	1
1	yellow onion, peeled & sliced	1
5	leeks, cleaned & sliced	5
1	whole garlic bulb, skins on individual cloves which are cut in half	1
3	bay leaves	3
5 mL	whole coriander seeds	1 tsp
3 mL	whole cumin seeds	½ tsp
5 mL	cayenne pepper sauce	1 tsp

| 185 mL | coconut milk | ¾ cup |
| 2 kg | cleaned steamer clams or mussels, in the shell | 4½ lbs |

With the exception of the last two items, place all ingredients in a large saucepan. Bring to the boil, reduce heat and simmer for 1 hour. Strain and discard pulp.

At this point the broth may be refrigerated overnight. When you are ready, warm the broth over medium heat. Add the coconut milk, stirring until broth comes to a gentle boil. Add the shellfish. Simmer for 5–10 minutes.

Serve immediately with thick chunks of warmed, sourdough bread. Encourage your diners to dunk salubriously in the addictive, briny nectar!

Clams: For another recipe using clams, see "Parsnips & Pasta" in Chapter Twelve, *Vegetables, Pies & Salads.*

DAVY JONES' LOCKER BIRD

**10 servings as hot appetizer, or
5 servings as entrée.**

*After nine days at sea, our depleted galley supplies was the
mother of this invention. When the skipper asked, "Where
did you get the vegetables?" I simply said, "Lean over and
look below."*

*There are many varieties of edible seaweed and reading suggestions are
given in the* References *at the end of this chapter. However, for the sake
of the 99.9 per cent who rely on a supermarket, I have listed the readily-
available nori in the ingredients.*

You also will need some kitchen twine and a pair of tongs.

*A final plea: do not throw away the supremely nutritious cooking water.
You can use it later as a base to make soup; as the water portion for
canned, condensed soup, or the liquid for a vegetable gelatin.*

500 g	ground turkey	1 lb
125 mL	wheat germ	½ cup
2	eggs	2
125 mL	buttermilk	½ cup
60 mL	chutney	¼ cup
5 mL	prepared minced garlic	1 tsp
5 mL	Dijon mustard	1 tsp
60 mL	dried coconut	¼ cup
1	stalk celery, very finely diced	1
1	10-sheet package of nori	1

Place all ingredients except the nori in a medium bowl and mix.

Place a sheet of nori on the diagonal on a cutting board, and drop
a large dollop of your mix on the corner nearest you. Roll up and

tuck the ends underneath. Take a generous length of string; double wrap across and around the newly-formed little maritime package. Tie a bow leaving long ends. Use a single knot because you want people to be able to unwrap your gifts easily at table.

Repeat for the other nine sheets.

Bring 3L (3 qts) water to boil in a 6L (6 qt) saucepan. Using tongs, arrange the ten green parcels in the boiling water. Cover, reduce heat and simmer for 35 minutes.

Using tongs, carefully remove each "Bird" from saucepan, and place directly onto individual plates.

Serve immediately with buttered lima beans or brown rice.

CHOPRA (reference at end of this chapter), a physician following Ayurvedic precepts, needs to know into which category a patient's mind/body type belongs before he is able to diagnose and/or prescribe. The three basic types are called Vata, Pitta and Kappa. As a layman I naïvely make a leap of analogy from this ancient East Indian paradigm to Sheldon's twentieth century Western idea which is based on the assumption of a physique/personality relationship falling into three main categories, *vis* endomorph, mesomorph and ectomorph. (There is considerable overlap in the paradigms' adjectival vocabularies in spite of eons between their formulation.) According to Chopra (pun most emphatically *not* intended), coconuts and the Pitta type (mesomorph?) belong together as:

1/ coconut is listed as a "Pitta-pacifying" food, and

2/ coconut is the preferred summer-time massage oil where Pitta dosha (the meeting point of mind to body) prevails (pp. 226–7 and 205).

FISH LOAF

6–7 servings

Egg plant (aubergine) as a predominant ingredient gives this dish its unusual flavor. The loaf lends itself either to dinner when served with vegetable accompaniments, or to an especially delectable, easy breakfast when served cold by itself. It is an ideal way to use large-fish leftovers.

375–500 mL	cooked fish, bones removed	1½–2 cups
400 g	small eggplant, diced	14 oz
1	small leek, thinly sliced	1
1	medium carrot, grated	1
5 mL	chopped garlic	1 tsp
15 mL	soy sauce	1 tbsp
125 mL	dried coconut	½ cup
3 mL	ground fennel seed	½ tsp
50 g	packet lemon dill sauce mix	1.8 oz
30 mL	coconut oil	2 tbsp
3	eggs	3
185 mL	rolled oats	¾ cup
185 mL	water	¾ cup

Pre-heat oven to 175°C (350°F).

Place all ingredients in a medium bowl. Mix thoroughly.

Pack into oiled loaf pan. Bake for 1–1¼ hours.

Serve warm, or refrigerate overnight and serve chilled.

FISH STEAKS, POACHED

3–4 servings

Poaching is the simplest method of preparing fish, yet one of the most versatile. Steaks or fillets may be used, and the method suits most varieties of fresh and saltwater species. Poached fish may be served hot or cold, with or without a sauce. Use this recipe as a baseline, then wander far and wide. Making coconut milk from powder is ideal for this dish. The fact that it is cheaper does not affect the calibre of the end product.

1	cross-cut, large halibut steak	1
250 mL	coconut milk	1 cup
125 mL	water	½ cup
3 mL	lemon pepper	½ tsp
5 mL	dill	1 tsp

Pre-heat oven to 180°C (350°F).

In a baking pan large enough to hold the steak flat, pour in the coconut milk and water. Sprinkle the lemon pepper.

Add the steak and sprinkle with dill. Cover. Cook in oven until flesh separates easily upon prodding with a fork. (Time will vary according to both the thickness and variety of steak: a piece of halibut 2 cm (¾–1") thick will take 20–25 minutes.)

Serve hot with a little of the broth and steamed vegetables; or serve chilled with a salsa (see Chapter Three, *Appetizers, Condiments & Savory Snacks*).

HALIBUT PAPILLOTE WITH VEGETABLE PURÉE

4 servings

This colorful meal is easy to prepare with ready-made phyllo. The nutritious purée can be made a day ahead and re-heated in a microwave just prior to serving.

Other "meaty" fish can be used instead of halibut. Skate and bass are good substitutes.

FOR THE PURÉE

2	large turnips	2
2	small beets	2
250 mL	coconut milk	1 cup
3 mL	garlic powder	½ tsp
5 mL	ground cumin	1 tsp
3 mL	black pepper	½ tsp

Place the turnips and beets in a saucepan. Cover with water and bring to boil. Reduce heat; simmer for 20–25 minutes. Drain off the cooking water. When cool enough to handle, peel the vegetables; cut in large chunks and place in food processor with the coconut milk and spices. Process until puréed. (If making ahead of time, transfer to a microwaveable dish and refrigerate.)

FOR THE PAPILLOTE

45 mL	olive oil	3 tbsp
375 mL	mushrooms, thinly sliced	1½ cups
30 mL	dried coconut	2 tbsp
1	red bell pepper, seeded & diced	1
3 mL	ground oregano	½ tsp

1	packet phyllo pastry	1
4	halibut steaks	4
2	limes, cut into 8 wedges	2

Garnish: sprigs of fresh watercress (or parsley).

Pre–heat oven to 200°C (400°F)

Over medium heat, warm the olive oil in a skillet. Add the mushrooms, coconut, bell pepper and oregano. Sauté for 5 minutes.

Grease a large baking pan.

Place 3 sheets of phyllo on a counter surface. Place a fish steak toward one side of the pastry. Spoon a quarter of the sauté mixture on top of the steak and roll up the pastry using an extra, folded phyllo sheet to patch any tears. Tuck the ends under and place papillote in baking pan. Repeat for the remaining 3 steaks. Bake for 20 minutes.

Place each papillote on a dinner plate and pour the red, vegetable purée to the side. Two lime wedges per plate plus watercress sprigs complete the colorful palette.

Serve immediately.

CHILD (reference at end of this chapter) believes the year 1841 marks the earliest patent for using coconut oil in the manufacture of soap. (It was claimed by R.L. Sturtevant: E.P.8870.) Popular demand for the ever-evolving, sophisticated, synthetic detergents over the last half-century has caused a dramatic decline in the use of coconut oil for soap-making. However, with the old wisdom of the market-place prevailing, sales continue to be steady both in areas where hard water prevails as well as in marine use due to its capability of lathering in seawater (pp. 164 and 173).

MACKEREL LUNCH

3 servings

A superior quality coconut milk (see Supply Sources *at the end of this book) is desirable for making this quick and economical dish. The powdered form may be substituted as long as all lumps are removed from the mix prior to adding other ingredients.*

398 mL	can coconut milk	14 liquid oz
425 g	can jack mackerel, drained & with bones removed	15 oz
1	small red chile pepper, seeded & diced	1
1	medium yellow onion, peeled & diced	1
3 mL	powdered ginger	½ tsp
8 mL	oregano OR	½ tbsp
15 mL	parsley	1 tbsp

Place all ingredients in a medium saucepan. Bring to a boil. Reduce heat. Simmer for 20 minutes, stirring occasionally.

Serve with toasted, multi-grain bagels.

NOT ANOTHER FISHY BREAKFAST?

2 servings

For breakfast I like seafood and I like pizza. This recipe gives me both. Try it just once for yourself. If it really does not suit your breakfast tastes, use it at another time of day served with a crisp green salad.

45 mL	coconut butter	3 tbsp
1	clove garlic, peeled & minced	1
3 mL	oregano	½ tsp
15 mL	red pepper sauce	1 tbsp
1	green onion, finely chopped	1
½	red or yellow bell pepper, seeded and diced	½
125 mL	mushrooms, diced	½ cup
106 g	can sardines, drained	3.75 oz
30 mL	fine dried coconut	⅛ cup
226 g	packet Boboli (with 2 shells)	8 oz
1–2 mL	lemon pepper	¼ tsp
125 mL	feta cheese, crumbled	½ cup

Pre-heat oven to 230°C (450°F).

In a small skillet, melt the coconut butter over medium heat. Add the garlic, oregano, red pepper sauce, green onion, bell pepper and mushrooms. Sauté for 8 minutes.

While the above is cooking, put the sardines and coconut into a small bowl. Mash together with the tines of a fork. Divide into two equal portions and pat firmly onto the centers of the pizza crusts. Sprinkle with lemon pepper.

Stir the sauté in skillet. Spread equal parts on the Boboli. Sprinkle with feta cheese. Oven bake for 8 minutes. Serve immediately.

POACHED SALMON WITH LIMA BEAN SAUCE: HOT

4 servings

Salmon is an ideal fish to poach because what you do not use immediately can be refrigerated to be served well-chilled the next day, either by itself or with a different sauce. (Sea bass may be substituted for this hot version of poached fish.) The cooking stock may also be used as the base for a sauce. (See next recipe, Poached Salmon With Velouté Sauce: Cold.*)*

Unless you have a proper fish poacher, you will need a length of cheese-cloth to prepare this dish.

FOR THE POACHED FISH:

1	large sweet, white onion, very finely diced	1
1	juice of lime	1
2 241 g	liquid from canned lima beans (see below)	2 8.5 oz
4	salmon fillets	4
2	limes, quartered	2
1½ L	water (or more as needed to later cover fillets in pan)	1 qt

FOR THE LIMA BEAN SAUCE:

2 241 g	cans lima beans (liquid kept for above)	2 8.5 oz
435 mL	coconut milk	1¾ cups
3 mL	dried dill	½ tsp
3 mL	chopped garlic	½ tsp
15 mL	hot pepper sauce	1 tbsp

| 15 mL | horseradish | 1 tbsp |
| 15 mL | cornstarch | 1 tbsp |

Prepare the poaching stock by placing the onion, lime juice, liquid from the lima beans and water into a large saucepan. Bring to a boil; reduce heat and simmer for 45 minutes. Strain and discard pulp.

Wrap the salmon in cheesecloth, all together or in 4 individual portions, securing each with an elastic band. Bring stock to boil again; lower wrapped fish into the stock, reduce heat and simmer for approximately 8 minutes. (The time will vary according to the thickness of the fillets. Be careful not to over-cook. Test with a fork: fish should flake when pierced gently.) Remove fish and place on serving platter. (Keep some of the stock for use in the next recipe. It may be kept in the freezer for as long as a week.)

While the fish is poaching, prepare the sauce:

Place all ingredients in a blender except the cornstarch. Purée. Add the cornstarch and blend. Transfer to a bowl or small saucepan and heat in the microwave or on the stove.

Place lime wedges by the salmon. Serve with boiled potatoes and pickled beets, with sauce on the table for self-service.

ERASMUS (reference at end of this chapter) maintains that an excellent tanning lotion can be made by mixing equal parts of coconut, walnut and flax oils. (Caution: flax oil does stain clothing.) He further recommends adding vitamin E and aloe vera. Quantities are not specified, nor is the level of protection. On the positive side, with this mixture one avoids chemicals, some of which reputedly become carcinogenic upon exposure to ultraviolet rays (p. 348).

POACHED SALMON WITH VELOUTÉ SAUCE: COLD

4 servings

"Velouté" is the chef's term for a thickened sauce made from fish stock. Here is a make-ahead dish which should be served very cold (although the sauce itself may be served hot).

FOR THE POACHED SALMON:

Prepare salmon according to directions in previous recipe. Refrigerate overnight.

FOR THE VELOUTÉ SAUCE:

45 mL	butter	3 tbsp
45 mL	flour	3 tbsp
15 mL	ranch-style salad dressing	1 tbsp
310 mL	strained poaching liquid (see previous recipe)	1¼ cups
185 mL	coconut milk	¾ cup
1 mL	nutmeg	¼ tsp
3 mL	curry powder	½ tsp
1–2 mL	sea-salt	¼ tsp
125 mL	fresh parsley, leaves only, finely chopped	½ cup

In a shallow saucepan, melt the butter. Stir in flour over medium heat; cook until blended and bubbly. Add, one at a time, the remaining ingredients except for the parsley. Cook, stirring continuously, until sauce has thickened. Add the parsley. Cook and stir for no longer than one minute more. Transfer to small serving-bowl and refrigerate.

Suggested serving: buffet-style with a selection of salads and a brioche loaf.

SHRIMP BOAT SALAD

4 servings

Cucumbers are used to make the hulls of these shrimp boats. If you feel like titivating with this luncheon dish, you can use wooden shish-ke-bab skewers to create masts rigged with white sails made from turnip slices or orange sails from carrots sliced on the diagonal.

2	cucumbers	2
500 mL	cooked baby shrimp	2 cups
125 mL	fresh or frozen (thawed) grated coconut	½ cup
125 mL	ranch-style dressing	½ cup
5 mL	dried dill	1 tsp
2	firm tomatoes, halved & thinly sliced	2

Cut cucumbers in half lengthwise. Strip a length from each curved side to allow the 4 halves to sit flat. Remove the seeds and pulp and place in a medium bowl. Put the cucumber halves on four luncheon plates, stripped side down. (They are now your hulls.)

To the pulp add the shrimp, coconut, ranch-style dressing and dill. Blend gently with a fork. Spoon equal quantities into the hulls. Arrange a row of tomato slices alongsides, or decorate nautically as you wish.

Serve immediately with chunks of French bread.

SHRIMP AND CORN PUDDING

4–5 servings

This dish can be prepared in the evening, stored in the refrigerator overnight, and baked in the morning for a hearty breakfast; or it may be cooked and served hot for a main meal. A crisp green salad is an excellent complement.

2	eggs	2
425 g	can cream-style corn	15 oz
80 mL	oil	¼ cup + 2 tbsp
125 mL	cheddar cheese, shredded	½ cup
60 mL	dried coconut	¼ cup
250 mL	yellow corn meal	1 cup
3 mL	hot pepper sauce	½ tsp
3 mL	baking powder	½ tsp
250 mL	raw shrimp, peeled & deveined	1 cup
1	medium onion, diced	1
1	green chile pepper, seeded & diced	1

Pre-heat oven to 175°C (350°F).

In a medium bowl, and using a wooden spoon, combine the eggs, corn and oil. One by one, stir in the remaining ingredients. Pour into a 20 x 20 cm (8" x 8") square oven dish. Bake for 50 minutes. Serve immediately.

Shrimp: For another recipe using shrimp, see "Pak Choi & Daikon Stir-Fry" in Chapter Twelve, *Vegetables, Pies & Salads*.

SOMETHING FISHY PATTIES

4 servings

It matters not whether your cooked fish is bluefish, salmon, mahi mahi, or red snapper, this "Something Fishy" recipe seems to work for many a variety and is an efficient use of leftovers.

For the seaweed, choose a dried, wispy thread or narrow strip variety. The color is not critical, and mixing types will not spoil the outcome.

750 mL	flaked, cooked fish	3 cups
125 mL	fine, dry breadcrumbs	½ cup
3	eggs, lightly beaten	3
8 mL	garlic powder	½ tbsp
5 mL	lemon pepper	1 tsp
3 mL	ground turmeric	½ tsp
125 mL	fresh or frozen shredded coconut	½ cup
125 mL	dried seaweed, cut into small flakes	½ cup
60 mL	flour	¼ cup
60 mL	coconut butter	¼ cup

In a large bowl, combine the fish, bread crumbs, eggs, garlic, lemon pepper, turmeric, coconut and seaweed. Mix with the hands until the ingredients hold together. (Hand blending is good for getting the right texture and for lifting the spirits.)

Form into 4 patties, thumb-thick at the centers and 4 finger widths across. Coat lightly with the flour.

In a skillet over medium heat, melt the coconut butter. Cook the patties for 4–5 minutes on both sides until golden.

For a complete meal, serve the patties hot with a spinach pasta, cole slaw on the side and lemon wedges.

Another option, and one which increased the overall test ratings from an 8 to a 10, is to refrigerate the Something Fishies overnight and serve cold with a good chutney for breakfast. Further, they are a welcome change from sandwiches for the lunchbox.

TUNA-SEA VEGETABLE MOUSSE

6 servings as entrée
12–14 servings as appetizer

The sea vegetable used in this prepare-ahead recipe is called hiziki. It grows on rocky ledges along the coast of Japan. The dried form required in this mousse usually comes in sealed packages of 60 g. Half a package of this size is sufficient. Take care to properly close and re-seal for the next use.

Hiziki seems to have a life of its own, even in dried form. As the recipe requires these bouncy little strands to be broken into much smaller lengths, I suggest placing them in a brown paper bag, twisting it closed, and pounding the bag with your fist or a mallet.

375 mL	water	1½ cups
30g	hiziki, strands broken (see above)	1 oz
2 170g	cans chunk light tuna, well-drained	6 oz
45 mL	prepared horseradish	3 tbsp
15 mL	pimiento, finely diced	1 tbsp
15 mL	lime juice	1 tbsp
8 mL	garlic powder	½ tbsp
8 mL	red pepper sauce	½ tbsp

3 mL	sea salt	½ tsp
8 mL	celery seed	½ tbsp
30 mL	gelatin powder	2 tbsp
100g	coconut powder	3.5 oz
250 mL	boiling water	1 cup

Oil a fish-mold or other 1½ L (1½ qt) metal pan. Set aside.

In a small saucepan measure 375 mL (1½ cups) water. Add the hiziki. Bring to a boil. Reduce heat and simmer for 10 minutes. Set aside.

In a medium-large bowl place the tuna, horseradish, pimiento, lime juice, garlic, red pepper sauce, sea salt and celery seed. Set aside.

Put the gelatin powder in a small jug and pour the cooking water from the hiziki onto them. With a teaspoon, stir until the gelatin has dissolved and all lumps are removed. Set aside to cool a little at room temperature.

Spoon the cooked, drained hiziki into the bowl holding the tuna and other ingredients.

Pour the coconut powder into a separate, medium bowl. Add the 250 mL (1 cup) boiling water to the powder and, with a wire whisk, whip vigorously until powder is completely dissolved. Add the now-setting gelatin to the creamy milk and whisk again until well-blended. Pour into the tuna bowl and stir all ingredients together with a wooden spoon until very well blended.

Transfer mixture to the oiled mold and refrigerate overnight.

When ready to serve, dip the bottom of the mold into a sink or pan of hot water for 20–30 seconds. Place a platter upside-down over the mold. Grasp the two together firmly and invert. The mousse should slither free, easily and intact. Surround with watercress or fresh spinach.

If using as a main dish, serve with chutney, a crunchy salad and slices of French bread.

If using as an appetizer, slice and place on cocktail-size slices of pumpernickel bread. If your presentation is particularly glorious, allow your guests to serve themselves and see how beautifully you have prepared this mousse.

REFERENCES AND SUGGESTED READING FOR CHAPTER ELEVEN

1. Udo Erasmus, *Fats That Heal, Fats That Kill.* Burnaby, BC. Alive Books. 1993, p. 348.

2. Deepak Chopra, MD, *Perfect Health: The Complete Mind/Body Guide.* New York, NY. Harmony Books. 1991, pp. 226–7 and p. 205.

3. Reginald Child, *Coconuts.* Tropical Agricultural Series. London, UK. Longmans, Green & Co. Ltd. 1964, pp. 164 and 173.

Szczawinski, A.F. & N.J. Turner. *Wild Green Vegetables of Canada.* Ottawa, Canada. National Museums of Canada. 1980.

Waaland, J.R. *Common Seaweeds of the Pacific Coast.* North Vancouver, BC. J.J. Douglas Ltd., 1977.

12

CAULIFLOWER WITH FETA CHEESE

7–9 servings as a meat accompaniment or
4–5 servings as main course

With a few extra touches, a lowly cauliflower is transformed into a sophisticated vegetable dish to accompany any of a variety of meats. It can also be served solo as a vegetarian luncheon with fresh brioche. Feta has a lower fat content than cheddar and brick cheeses.

1	small cauliflower, broken into flowerets	1
1	equal or lesser amount of broccoli, broken into flowerets	1
125 mL	dried coconut flakes	½ cup
60 mL	almond flakes	¼ cup
15 mL	lemon juice	1 tbsp
23 mL	tamari- or soy sauce	1½ tbsp
3 mL	ground turmeric	½ tsp
140 g	feta cheese, crumbled	5 oz

Pre-heat oven to 150°C (300°F).

Steam cauliflower and broccoli together for 8 minutes. Drain well and transfer to an oven-to-table dish.

While the vegetables are steaming, toast the coconut and almond flakes in a microwave on high setting for 30 seconds. Stir the flakes, and microwave for another 30 seconds.

Sprinkle the lemon juice on the vegetables and then the tamari or soy sauce.

Distribute the combined coconut and almond flakes over the food, followed by the crumbled feta cheese.

Bake for 15 minutes, or until topping is a light, golden brown. (Take care to avoid burning the cheese topping.) Serve immediately.

FESTIVE MARMALADE SWEET POTATOES

8 servings

To enhance the attractiveness of this vegetable delight, select the dark-orange variety of sweet potato over the yellow.

This colorful, festive dish has a special affinity for roast pork, duck or turkey. It keeps well in the refrigerator if prepared a day or two ahead of time. Re-heat gently in your conventional oven or microwave.

2	large orange sweet potatoes, peeled and diced	2
2 mL	pepper	¼ tsp
3 mL	coriander	½ tsp
250 mL	ginger or orange marmalade	1 cup
185 mL	coconut milk	¾ cup

Steam the sweet potatoes until soft. Drain and place in large mixing bowl. Add remaining ingredients. With electric mixer, blend on slow speed until you have a thick purée. This does not have to be lump-free, just well-blended.

Transfer to a serving-bowl and serve immediately, or cover and refrigerate overnight. Heat before serving.

(Although this dish may be eaten cold, its rich taste and texture are definitely superior if warmed.)

HEARTS OF PALM SALAD

4 servings

To each coconut tree there is only one heart. A dish made of this tropical delicacy is consequently on the costly side, unless you are able to glean for yourself. For more information, see "Hearts of Palm" in Chapter Two, Coconuts and Health.

Hearts of palm are white and available in cans from specialty food stores. Arranged in a wide, wooden bowl on a quiet, green background, they look especially inviting.

1	bunch fresh spinach, thick stems removed	1
425 g	can asparagus spears, drained	15 oz
1	stalk celery, very finely diced	1
1	kiwi, peeled and sliced	1
398 mL	can hearts of palm, drained and cut into thick, diagonal slices	14 liquid oz
125 mL	creamy cucumber salad dressing	½ cup

In a serving bowl, place a bed of washed spinach. Arrange the asparagus spears in spoke-wheel formation. Add the celery, kiwi and hearts of palm.

Use the dressing to complete the wheel effect by making a strong center circle and a thin outer one. Serve.

JAY AND THE GIANT ZUCCHINI

6–8 servings

You may have guessed from the title that there is a story coming? You are right. Jay and I were hired as colleagues on the same day, little knowing that the following twenty years would see us still working together. As office mates, and later office neighbors, we have seen each other's families take shape, evolve, and change into another generation. Many memories have accrued. One such whimsy was that early in September of each year I would receive a giant squash. Later in September, he and his lovely wife would host their annual zucchini party.

The party-goers brought their biggest and best for judgment. As the critical deliberations progressed, libations flowed, causing the critiques to be accompanied by the occasional wee bit of vulgarity. The downside of all this frivolity was the sotto voce *complaints about what to do with the things. After all, just one of them lasted forever . . . well, two weeks anyway! What follows is a solution, dedicated to my dear friend.*

1	giant zucchini	1
30 mL	coconut butter	2 tbsp
4	drops chile oil	4
8 mL	granulated garlic	½ tbsp
1	large yellow onion, diced	1
1	red bell pepper, seeded and diced	1
60 mL	dried coconut	¼ cup
15 mL	sesame seeds	1 tbsp
225 g	feta cheese, crumbled	8 oz
2 283 g	packages frozen chopped spinach, thawed	2 10 oz

FOR THE SAUCE:

2 284 mL	cans condensed green pea soup	2 10 oz	
1	can water	1	
3 mL	black pepper	½ tsp	

Pre-heat oven to 175°C (350°).

Find your largest baking or roasting pan. Cut your giant zucchini at the stalk end to fit into pan. Remove from pan, and slice off lengthwise the top third of the squash. Set aside. Remove the pith and seeds and discard. Return squash to pan and set aside.

In a small skillet, warm the coconut butter, chile oil, and garlic. Add the onion and bell pepper. Sauté for 3 minutes, or until translucent.

Transfer skillet's entire contents into a medium bowl. Add the coconut, sesame seeds, feta cheese, and spinach. Blend well with a wooden spatula. Stuff this mix into the hollowed squash. Use the third you removed as a lid. Press down to seal the edges together firmly. If there is any slack in the "lid" or in the pan, secure zucchini with skewers.

Bake for 1¼–1¾ hours (depending on size). The flesh should be slightly firm, but not hard.

A couple of minutes before removing squash from the oven, bring the soup, water, and pepper to boil in a medium saucepan, stirring continuously.

Cut the stuffed squash into hand-width slices. Place on individual plates. Pour the pea sauce on top. Serve.

MUSHROOMS WITH TAHINI SAUCE

4 servings as one-dish meal or
8–10 servings as accompaniment to entrée.

This simple yet unusual dish may be served as a satisfying vegetarian entrée entire unto itself, or as an accompaniment to another main-course item. As it is best eaten as soon as prepared, I find it tastier as a main course.

221 g	package bean threads (saifun)	8 oz
30 mL	of the separated oil from top of tahini jar OR butter	2 tbsp
500–700 g	mushrooms, washed and sliced to 1 cm thickness	1–1½ lb
8 mL	chopped garlic	½ tbsp
3 mL	pepper	½ tsp
3 mL	salt, optional	½ tsp
113 g	tahini (raw, ground sesame seeds)	½ cup
310 mL	coconut milk	1¼ cups
2	bunches watercress, washed and with thick base of stems removed	2

Prepare the bean threads as directed on package. Take care not to overcook: one minute at full boil is usually ample. Set aside to drain fully.

With a little of the separated oil (or butter), sauté the mushrooms for 5–10 minutes with garlic and pepper. Do not overcook or the mushrooms will be soggy. Transfer mushrooms to a large serving platter, mounding them in the center.

Arrange the drained bean-threads around the mushrooms, creating a high bank to contain the tahini sauce. If desired, sprinkle the salt.

To the same pan in which the mushrooms were cooked, add the tahini and coconut milk. With a wooden spoon, and using medium heat, stir constantly until a smooth, creamy sauce is formed. Pour over mushrooms.

Arrange watercress abundantly in an outer ring and serve immediately.

Soy sauce makes a piquant table condiment for this dish.

Variation: Tahini cooked with coconut milk in the same proportions as above also makes a pleasant and easy-to-prepare sauce to top a medley of steamed vegetables. Try it, for example, with a mix of cauliflower, carrots and snow peas.

ONION PIE

4–6 servings

A wire whisk and a wooden spoon are the mixing tools of choice for this vegetarian dish. It is best served directly from the oven.

1	basic pie dough (home or store-bought)	1
60 mL	butter	¼ cup
3	large sweet, white onions, sliced	3
2	eggs	2
250 mL	coconut milk	1 cup
30 mL	flour	2 tbsp
3 mL	lemon pepper	½ tsp
2 mL	nutmeg	¼ tsp
5 mL	chopped parsley	1 tsp
250 mL	sharp cheddar cheese, shredded	1 cup
1	medium tomato, sliced	1

Pre-heat oven to 175°C (350°F).

Place prepared pie dough in a deep-dish pie pan, and bake for 5 minutes only. Remove from oven and increase temperature to 190°C (375°F).

Sauté onions in butter over low heat until translucent and golden.

In a separate bowl mix eggs, coconut milk, flour and spices. Add onions and cheese. Stir gently, then pour into pie crust. Garnish with tomato. Bake for 30 minutes. Serve.

PAK (BOK) CHOI AND DAIKON STIR-FRY

4–6 servings

Here is a quick meal which is texturally different. A wok is best for any stir-fry, but a large skillet will suffice.

60 mL	olive oil	¼ cup
60 mL	soy sauce	¼ cup
5 mL	chile oil (or red pepper sauce)	1 tsp
2 mL	ground turmeric	¼ tsp
5 mL	garlic powder	1 tsp
4 cm	piece fresh ginger, peeled and grated	1½"
700 g	fresh pak choi, rinsed and cut into 2 cm wide strips	1½ lbs
225 g	daikon (Japanese radish), cut in 1 cm pieces	½ lb
60 mL	fresh or frozen coconut, grated	¼ cup
1	small, yellow chile pepper, seeded and diced	1
250 mL	mushrooms, washed and halved	1 cup

Optional: 2 cups shrimp, shelled and de-veined
Topping: sesame seeds

Place first three ingredients in a wok or large skillet, and heat at medium setting. Add remaining items in order listed. With a spatula, turn contents occasionally until cooked to desired consistency, but not more than 10 minutes.

Serve immediately with steamed rice. Provide sesame seeds as a table condiment.

PARSNIPS AND PASTA

4 servings

For cooks perplexed by a diner's "attitude" toward vegetables, here is a suggestion. Use a different title for this meal —perhaps simply "fettuccini." The parsnip sauce may be made ahead of time, refrigerated overnight, and re-heated in the microwave.

FOR THE SAUCE:

500 g	parsnips	1¼ lbs
3 mL	kelp (or sea salt)	½ tsp
3 mL	ground nutmeg	½ tsp
5 mL	powdered ginger	1 tsp
125 mL	coconut milk	½ cup
125 mL	water	½ cup

Peel parsnips; remove and discard the stalk ends and cut roots into bite-size chunks. (If you purchased the large, thick variety, slice them lengthwise and excise the triangular, pithy core found at the stalk end.)

Steam parsnips for 10–12 minutes, drain, and transfer to a food processor. Add remaining ingredients and purée. Sauce is now ready for serving on top of the pasta, or you may refrigerate for later use.

FOR THE PASTA:

1	package spinach fettuccini	1
1	small, red chile, seeded and finely diced	1
184 g	can chopped clams, drained	6½ oz
30 mL	virgin olive oil or butter	2 tbsp

Prepare pasta according to directions on package, taking care not to overcook. Drain. Add remaining ingredients, stirring gently to mix evenly.

Serve immediately with the warmed parsnip sauce.

Optional topping: parmesan cheese.

Variation: The above parsnip purée may be used as a sauce to top a medley of colorful, steamed vegetables. Suggestions are:

1. Broccoli, carrots, and eggplant

2. Tomatoes, onions, and peas

3. Cauliflower, bell peppers, and beets

POTATO-CHEESE CASSEROLE

5–7 servings

Although a delight to the palate when served direct from the oven, the rave reviews on this one will be more generous if you take a minute to garnish the dish for color en route *to the table: an edible flower or two, a few slices of tomato, or even some good old parsley sprigs.*

5	large potatoes	5
3	medium white onions	3
1	small, red chile pepper, seeded and finely diced	1
15 mL	tamari sauce	1 tbsp
3 mL	lemon pepper	½ tsp
250 mL	coconut milk	1 cup

2 mL	ground nutmeg	¼ tsp
250 mL	grated Myzithra cheese	1 cup
	(feta may be substituted,	
	but it alters the texture)	

Pre-heat oven to 200°C (400°F).

Place unpeeled potatoes and peeled onions in a large saucepan, cover with water, and bring to a boil. Reduce heat to medium, and cook for 9–10 minutes. Drain water. When vegetables are cool enough to handle, cut into 1 cm (½") slices.

In a large oven-to-table casserole, arrange half the potato slices. Follow this with a layer of all the onion slices. Distribute the diced chili over all. Sprinkle with tamari sauce and lemon pepper.

Arrange the second half of the potato slices, and shake the nutmeg evenly on top.

Spoon the Myzithra cheese over the entire surface.Gently pour the coconut milk in even distribution over the vegetables, and place casserole in oven for 25 minutes, or until gloriously golden. Serve hot.

RUTABAGA PIE

5–7 servings

If you have to prepare the family meal after spending a day at work, I suggest you cook the rutabagas and parsnips in this recipe the previous evening while you have another meal underway. Then this pie is an easy yet impressive meal to prepare.

2	medium rutabagas, boiled, peeled and diced	2
2	parsnips, boiled, peeled and diced	2
3 mL	garlic powder	½ tsp
8 mL	parsley flakes	½ tbsp
60 mL	dried coconut	¼ cup
227 g	can mushroom stems and pieces, drained, reserve liquid	8 oz
1	medium sweet, white onion, diced	1
375 mL	frozen broccoli pieces, thawed	1½ cups
30 mL	coconut butter, softened	2 tbsp
3 mL	ground turmeric	½ tsp
3 mL	mustard powder	½ tsp
60 mL	mushroom brine (see above)	¼ cup
227 g	low-fat cream cheese	8 oz
2 mL	black pepper	¼ tsp

FOR THE TOPPING:

375 mL	baking (biscuit) mix	1½ cups
125 mL	buttermilk	½ cup

Pre-heat oven to 190°C (375°F).

Boil the rutabagas and parsnips for 10 minutes. When cool enough to handle, peel, dice, and place in bottom of a 2L (2qt) casserole. Sprinkle the garlic, parsley, and coconut on top.

In layers, add the mushrooms, onion, and broccoli respectively. Drop the coconut butter in little blobs over all. Sprinkle with the turmeric, mustard powder, and mushroom liquid.

Distribute the cream cheese in small chunks, and sprinkle the pepper on top.

In a separate, small bowl, mix the biscuit mix and buttermilk. Spoon the dough onto the vegetable casserole. Bake 35–40 minutes, or until crust is a dark, golden color.

May be served immediately or kept warm for an hour.

SMOKY PEPPER AND MUSHROOM SALAD

4–6 servings

This unusual salad is somewhat fussy to prepare but has the advantage of improving overnight in the refrigerator, provoking intrigued comments from appreciative guests. Searing of the skins of the bell peppers forces their oils into the flesh, thereby imparting the distinctive flavor of this dish. Long-handled tongs and an oven mitt are necessities.

You will need an open flame. A gas stove is ideal, but you may use a camping cooker, propane barbeque, or even a blow torch.

1	large lime	1
1 kilo	small, white mushrooms with lower parts of stems removed	2¼ lbs
2	red bell peppers, seared, skinned, and cut into thin strips	2
125 mL	fresh or frozen (thawed) coconut, grated	½ cup
125 mL	feta cheese, crumbled	½ cup

FOR THE DRESSING

125 mL	olive oil	½ cup
60 mL	red basil vinegar	¼ cup
5 mL	garlic powder	1 tsp
2 mL	black pepper	¼ tsp
5 mL	prepared horseradish	1 tsp
10 mL	prepared mustard	2 tsp

Into a large pot of water add the lime juice and lime peels. Bring to a boil.

Add the mushrooms and cook for 4–5 minutes. Drain, and set aside.

Using tongs, firmly hold a bell pepper over open flame until the skin is blistered to a light brown color. Rotate the pepper over the flame until all the skin is blistered. Set aside, and sear the second pepper. When peppers are cool enough to handle, remove skins by scraping or pulling (they should come off easily). Discard pith and seeds. Slice the aromatic flesh.

Into a large serving-bowl place the mushrooms, pepper, coconut and cheese. Mix together gently with the fingers.

In a small mixing-bowl place all the dressing ingredients, and blend thoroughly with a small, wire whisk. Pour over salad.

Cover and refrigerate until ready to serve. This salad partners meatier fish such as sturgeon, bass, and turbot. (Canada Fisheries, I'm behind you all the way!) Or it may be served by itself with a light brioche.

TORTELLINI WITH CHINESE PEA PODS

2 servings

There is no need to make accompaniments to this meal. It is a hearty, vegetarian dinner, entire unto itself. However, if served with bread or rolls, the quantity is adequate for a threesome lunch.

255 g	package fresh spinach tortellini	9 oz
15 mL	coconut oil	1 tbsp
23 mL	soy sauce	1½ tbsp
15 mL	hot pepper sauce	1 tbsp
2	cloves garlic, peeled and sliced	2
310 mL	sliced mushrooms	1¼ cups
5 mL	parsley flakes	1 tsp
227 mL	can bamboo shoots, drained	8 liquid oz
170 g	package frozen Chinese pea pods, thawed	6 oz
½	carrot, grated	½
60 mL	fresh or frozen grated coconut	¼ cup

Topping: sesame seeds as a table condiment

In a large saucepan, bring 2L (2qt) water to boil. Add the tortellini, and cook for 7 minutes (or according to package directions). Drain. Keep warm.

In a large skillet heat the coconut oil, being careful not to burn. Add garlic slices and cook for 2–3 minutes, turning with a spatula.

Add all remaining ingredients except the coconut. Stir-fry for 5 minutes, turning the vegetables occasionally. Add the coconut. Cook for another 2 minutes. Combine the skillet's contents with the waiting tortellini. Blend gently with a wooden spoon.

Transfer to dining plates. Serve immediately. Sesame seeds may be added at the table.

VEGETABLE MOUSSE

4–5 servings

To achieve a touch of festivity for commonplace vegetables, this gelatin-based dish is hard to beat for its quick and inexpensive qualities. It lends itself to microwave preparation, so instructions are in this medium, but by all means use a saucepan if you prefer.

398 mL	can coconut milk	1¾ cups
23 mL	gelatin granules	1½ tbsp
310 mL	colorful, frozen vegetables, thawed and diced	1¼ cups
1	stalk celery, very finely diced	1
3 mL	poppy seeds	½ tsp

Pour the coconut milk into a medium size bowl. Microwave until hot (time varies, but 2 minutes should be enough in most models). Add the gelatin and blend briskly with wire whisk, making sure all lumps are removed.

Stir in vegetable mix and celery. Allow to sit for 15 minutes. Sprinkle poppy seeds on top. Refrigerate for 2–3 hours, or until set. Ideal accompaniment to baked fish, or serve as children's mid-morning snack.

VEGETABLE SALAD

5–7 servings

For a departure from leafy salads, here is one which is easy to prepare and made from readily-available ingredients.

2	large carrots, grated	2
300 g	mushrooms, stalks discarded, sliced	11 oz
398 mL	can unsalted peas, drained	14 oz
125 mL	fresh or frozen shredded coconut	½ cup
15 mL	lime juice	1 tbsp
185 mL	Italian dressing	¾ cup
3 mL	dill weed	½ tsp

In a medium bowl place all ingredients in sequence listed. Mix lightly, and serve.

YULETIDE SNOW SCENE

Sales of coconut are at their peak around Christmas time. Coconut is snow on many confections, but it is seldom used as vegetable decoration. To rectify this circumstance, I conclude with a proposal that you make a beautiful, edible, salad table-piece for the holiday season.

The base in which you make your arrangement is significant. I use a large, shallow, wooden bowl. A white, oval quiche dish suffices. Use any bowl or rimmed plate with a large, flat base.

Dare to be different! Do you want an icy lake? Try blue-cheese dressing. A rocky hill? Walnuts. Stumps? Mushrooms. Igloos? Inverted coconut half-shells. A log cabin? Celery stalks, asparagus spears. With a roof? Grape leaves, spinach. A bench? Potato wedges. A wood pile? Carrot sticks. Some conifers? Carved aubergine (eggplant), stubby cucumber. A garden path? A fence? An animal? A wagon wheel? A wheelbarrow? Have fun, fun, fun!

For the final touch: sprinkle your wintry scene with pristine, shredded coconut snow.

This is art. Feel free to ad-lib! If creativity is not your forte, simply assume a Mona Lisa smile when receiving your applause. Be proud. Be triumphant. Exclaim your kitchen's new slogan: COCONUTS FOREVER!

METRIC CONVERSION CHART
FOR THE MEASURES MOST FREQUENTLY USED IN THIS BOOK.

1 L	4½ cups
250 mL	1 cup
125 mL	½ cup
60 mL	¼ cup
15 mL	1 tablespoon
5 mL	1 teaspoon
3 mL	½ teaspoon
2 mL	¼ teaspoon
1 mL	⅛ teaspoon
1 k	2.24 pounds
454 g	16 ounces
28 g	1 ounce
245°C	475°F
225°C	425°F
205°C	400°F
190°C	375°F
175°C	350°F
165°C	325°F
150°C	300°F

ANNOTATED BIBLIOGRAPHY

These books are about coconuts and/or lipids. References to other topics (such as seaweeds) are to be found at the end of Chapters Two and Eleven.

Child, Reginald, BSc, PhD, FRIC, *Coconuts.* Longmans, Green and Co. Ltd., London, 1964. My unreserved compliment is that this is the most concise, knowledgeable and comprehensive writing on coconuts. It covers such diverse topics as historical background, geography, industry, commercial products, botany, plantations, pests, crops and domestic applications. Woodroof (see below) accords him several citations. I sought to obtain permission to quote Child directly, but publishing companies have gone through stressful times in the past couple of decades. Owing to amalgamations and buy-ups, my quest proved to be unfruitful. However, most of the larger libraries still have a couple of copies on the shelf. The reward of procuring one justifies the endeavor.

Enig, Mary G., Ph.D. *Know Your Fats: The Complete Primer for Understanding the Nutrition of Fats, Oils, and Cholesterol.* Bethesda Press, Silver Spring, MD, 2000. The essential reference for every person working in the healing arts and sciences. Enig writes with clarity, authority, and awesome detail. I like to think of her as The Queen of Lipids. If you buy only one healthcare resource book, make it this one.

Erasmus, Udo, *Fats That Heal, Fats That Kill,* revised ed., Alive Books, Burnaby, BC, 1993. I surmise that Udo Erasmus is the person who most has heightened public awareness concerning the role of fats in health and disease. He must be a man of abundant energy and commitment. Over several years he has gathered and synthesized enormous quantities of data to present his ideas and findings to the general consumer. He writes in an affable, journalistic style. My single reservation is that he seldom gives page numbers to references which are supposed to be specific.

Fife, Bruce, N.D., *The Healing Miracles of Coconut Oil,* 2nd ed., HealthWise, Colorado Springs, CO, 2001. A digestible little book, written for the layman, summarizing the health values of coconut. The reader is in for some pleasant surprises and useful applications. Be sure to get the second edition. It is superior to the first.

Finnegan, John, *The Facts About Fats: A Consumer's Guide To Good Oils.* Elysian Arts, Malibu, CA, 1992. A forerunner to the new attitudes on fats, Finnegan's '92 edition is smaller and bolder than the 1993 Celestial Arts version. It is now hard to find, but worth usedbookstore browsing—especially if you like the "in-a-nutshell" category of literature.

Siguel, Edward N., MD, PhD, *Essential Fatty Acids in Health and Disease.* Nutrek Press, Brookline, MA, 1994. Reading this book is as essential to understanding disease prevention as essential fatty acids are to health. Dr. Siguel is a man of integrity and science who writes with grace. He transmutes the complex into the simple, without being simplistic. Highly recommended.

Wallach, Joel D., BS, DVM, ND, and Ma Lan, MD, MS, *Rare Earths: Forbidden Cures,* 2nd ed., Double Happiness Publishing Co., Bonita, CA, 1995. I include Wallach in this bibliography for reason of his Chapter Eight's implied information regarding fats' role in human life. (He favors minerals as the key to good health.) The author has a lucid, authoritative and humorous style. He gives the diets of the eight cultures most frequently described and studied for their trait of longevity. (Their peoples tend to die at a *healthy* old age.) One glance at the foods' list makes our comestible horrors seem contrived: whole milk, cheeses, organ meats fried in ghee and tallow. . . . Perhaps it is the relaxed attitude towards eating all foods available which makes this portion of the book such delightful reading.

Woodroof, Jasper Guy, PhD, *Coconuts: Production, Processing, Products*. Major Feed and Food Crops in Agriculture and Food Series. The Avi Publishing Company Inc., Westport, CT, 1970. A precise, scholarly text elaborating the subjects of its title exactly. If you seek hard data, this is the book.

SUPPLY SOURCES

A

AGAR AGAR. Shop for this at an Asian grocery store in the sea-weed (or sea-vegetable) section. It comes packaged in several forms: shredded, powdered (crystals) or compacted, rectangular blocks. Most common package sizes are 14 g and 42.5 g (.5oz and 1.5oz respectively).

B

BART SPICES LTD have five coconut products of consistently good quality. Their distribution is limited to the United Kingdom and Barbados. Items are Creamed Coconut (i.e. in block form for grating according to quantity needed), Coconut Cream (in tetrapacks), Organic Coconut Milk, their standard Coconut Milk, and 88% Fat Free Coconut Milk.

BOB'S RED MILL. As its name suggests, this company specializes in grains and flours. Their difference is that their farinaceous items are all organic. They stock both sweetened and unsweetened dried coconut in assorted shred sizes and shapes. They are in process of coming around to trusting the nature of coconut's saturated fat so that I suspect they will soon stock food grade coconut oil. They are located in a park-like setting; run a snack bar with wholesome foods, and also boast a book section for special diets. One is encouraged to browse. A visit is a mini stress-break. They fill mail orders, domestic and international. Write, fax, phone or visit 5209 S.E. International Way, Milwaukee, OR 97222, tel. 503-654-3215, fax 503-653-1339.

BUKO is the soft, jelloid meat of the young coconut. It is seldom cooked, for it has a delicate flavor which is easily lost. Unless you are fortunate enough to be on a palm-clad beach where coconuts are there for the picking, frozen buko is your best option. Simex or Filtaste are good brands among several others. Frozen buko is available at most Asian markets, or see "Caribbean & Newfoundland Market" below.

C

CARIBBEAN AND NEWFOUNDLAND MARKET: the site of the loving labors of wife and husband team Savi (introduced in the recipe for "Irish Moss Shake" in Chapter Six, *Drinks, Confections & Ice Creams*) & John Robbins. Savi is from Trinidad and John, Nova Scotia. The mix of foods from the Caribbean and the Maritimes, their respective homelands, is awesome and not as strange a combination as one would at first suspect. Both countries were part of the Commonwealth, along with Africa, sharing England as their rapacious mother country. Their history of exchanging foods dates back to the slave trade of the seventeenth century. Slaves had to be fed, albeit in sub-standard fashion. Prior to refrigeration, salting meat and fish was the common practice. The salted foods kept well and were very cheap. The Maritimes traded salt cod, herring, salmon, beef and pork for rum and molasses. Newfoundland hard breads are found in the Caribbean in slightly altered form. England's sweets (candies) are similarly known all over the Commonwealth. In October, 1999, Savi's brother and sister, Kris and Roma, took over responsibility for the store. They are just as friendly and welcoming as its owners.

For me, a trip to the Caribbean Market cum socio-cultural center assumes the aura of a magical pilgrimage. They stock every conceivable coconut item at a competitive price. They sell exotic spices, strange dried things, sauces for little-known dishes, canned tropical fruits, soup mixes and dried seaweeds. Besides running the retail outlet, they are also wholesalers and manufacturers. Mail orders, including C.O.D., are accepted. Write 1003 Royal Avenue, New Westminster, BC, Canada, V3M 1KO, or tel/fax 1-604-522-9480.

If you are in the area, do pay them a visit and tell them your discovery was through this book.

CHESTNUT PUREE. Purchase in European-style delicatessen. Usually comes in small cans or jars. The sugar-free brands are by far the best buy.

COCONUT. Grows on the *Cocus nucifera* variety of palm tree. It is to be found on many tropical and sub-tropical beaches as well as in the produce department of grocery stores. The latter seldom has large ones and their coconut water content is often minimal—or completely dried up. One import company, Melissa's Brand, incises a groove around the circumference of the coconut making it easy to break open. (Their coconuts are easy to spot with a sticker placed on each drupe. The sticker's logo sports a bright-orange carrot for the 'i' of its name. I don't want to know why.)

COCOA POWDER. See "Pure cocoa powder" below.

COCONUT CREAM is the first skim from the top of the pan in the process of making coconut milk. It has a thicker consistency. (If using the better brands of coconut milk one is hard put to tell the difference between the two.) Fiesta's cream is excellent.

COCONUT CREAM POWDER. Home Gourmet is a good brand which comes in convenient-size foil packs. However, coconut milk powder (see below) is often easier to find and a good substitute. To obtain cream consistency, simply mix a larger amount of powder to the water.

COCONUT EXTRACT. See "imitation coconut extract" below.

COCONUT MILK. Although it is quite fun to make your own milk from fresh coconuts, more than nine out of ten cooks prefer to purchase the canned variety. Quality varies enormously from brand to brand and unfortunately cannot be spotted logically by the price tag. A poor product can ruin a good meal. My favorites for quality consistency include Blue Orchid, Fiesta, A Taste of Thai, and Aroy-D. The latter offers the convenience of small cans of 156 mL (5.6 fl.oz). The standard size is 398 mL (14 fl.oz).

COCONUT MILK POWDER should be readily-available in supermarkets, but surprisingly often is not. It is space-saving, economical and has a long shelf-life. Ask the manager to stock it. Your request would be entirely reasonable. Many of the smaller ethnic stores carry a couple of product lines. Nestlé's (also known under the Maggi label in Canada and parts of the United States) and Fiesta are two consistently good brands.

COCONUT OIL. Make sure you purchase a food grade oil. Even health food stores often stock a cosmetic grade under the guise of food. Check the small print. Omega Nutrition produces an excellent brand, called Coconut Butter™. Ask your local health food store to stock it. For more details, see 'Omega' below. The company's products are also available in the U.S.A. (For a medium chain triglyceride (MCT) derivative, see 'MCT' below.)

COCONUT SYRUP. There are many brands available which are sold in supermarkets. It is a matter of locating them. The cans are usually small and often shelved with such drink mixes as piña colada. They are high in sugar content and often bound with emulsifying stabilizers and added flavor. The syrup contained in glass, or more often, plastic bottles for pouring over pancakes can sometimes be found with pancake and biscuit mixes. Cappucino bars stock a more expensive variety for flavoring coffees and milks. Of these I favor Torani. You can make your own syrup: see "Baked Pancake" in Chapter Four, *Breads, Coffee Cakes, Pancakes & Cookies.*

COCONUT WATER (often erroneously called "milk"). This is the rich-in-potassasium-and-enzymes liquid within the fresh, whole coconut. Of the commercial brands my favorite is Fiesta. It comes in a cardboard 250 mL (8½ fl.oz) carton with drinking-straw attached, and is available in many ethnic grocery stores. I have bought discounted crates way beyond (by a year) the expiration date and found only two cartons that had gone sour. It is produced by Fresh Fruit Drinks Inc., 1052 EDSA, Makati, Metro Manila, Philippines.

COMMUNITY FOOD CO-OP lies south of the border in Bellingham, WA. It is a large coöp which stocks many health and imported foods. They have especially good lines of oils (including the Omega Nutrition Canada Inc. products mentioned under 'coconut oil' above). They are located at 1220 North Forest. They do not fill mail orders but are willing to check their existing supplies for you in response to telephone enquiry. The number is 360-734-8158.

CREAMED COCONUT. See KTC creamed coconut below.

D

DAL is not always easy to find in the average grocery store unless you live in a district which has an East Indian population. It is sometimes sold in the bulk bins section. A wide range of dal products is usually available in ethnic specialty shops. G.S. Teja Ltd. is a family-run import business which puts out a good line. They are located in Richmond, BC. Fax 604-273-7534.

DRIED COCONUT is the most commonly used form of coconut for home baking. It is partially dried (most often by 30% oil reduction) before packaging. Supermarkets tend to stock more of the sweetened than unsweetened variety. Take special note in this regard as none of the recipes in this book calls for the sweetened version. Some markets stock their sweetened packages in the "Baking Needs" aisle, leaving the unsweetened for the self-serve bulk bins. If you do not find your requirements met, place a request. This is not a difficult product for your store's buyer to obtain.

DULSE. Packages of dried dulse are often placed by the fresh fish in your regular supermarket.

F

FAMOUS FOODS. This store is known for its natural foods as well as a wonderful selection of imported items. They stock all varieties of coconut products except fresh frozen. Address is 1595 Kingsway (at King Edward Avenue), Vancouver, BC, Canada, V5N 2R8. They welcome mail orders, both domestic and foreign. The manager asks that you have your credit card to hand when you call, tel. 1-604-872-3019.

FRESHLY GRATED (SHREDDED) COCONUT. To obtain the meat from picked or purchased coconuts, see pp. xii–xiii "To Open a Coconut."

FROZEN GRATED CASSAVA is usually available alongside frozen grated coconut. See next item.

FROZEN GRATED COCONUT may be found in the freezer section of Caribbean and Asian grocery stores. It usually comes in clear, plastic packages of 454 g (16 oz). To date I have not found frozen grated coconut in even the larger food stores. However, if you are likely to be a frequent user and you shop in an ethnic community, have a chat with the store manager. There are several good brands. The easiest to find on the west coast is Orient's Delight processed by Cathay Pacific Multi-Commodities Corp., 17 Clemente Street, Bgy.San Agustin, Novaliches, Quezon City, Philippines.

G

GARAM MASALA is available in East Indian and Asian markets in the spices section. A reputable import company is G.S. Teja Ltd. of Richmond, BC. Fax 604-273-7534.

GYOZA WRAPS. Seek in the refrigerator section of an Asian market or in the Asian section of the large supermarkets.

H

HIZIKI is a Japanese seaweed so rich in health-giving nutrients that it is often recommended for pregnant women. Somewhat difficult to find in Canada, but invariably stocked by Uwajimaya Inc. For more details, see under 'U' below.

I

IMITATION COCONUT EXTRACT. Coconut extract is invariably "imitation" as the flavor and aroma are chemically synthesized. Extracts are located with the herbs and spices in your regular grocery store. Brands most likely to be found in Canada are Blue Ribbon, French's, and Schwartz. In my opinion they are all at par.

IRISH MOSS is available in the stores which sell a wide variety of dried seaweeds. See also "Caribbean and . . ." above. The moss usually comes in 27 g packets (.95 oz). Please note that it must be strained after cooking.

J

J.B. FOODS, a grocery store which does not fill mail orders or appreciate telephone enquiries, but *is* open seven days a week from 10:30 a.m. to 6:00 p.m. The owner is both gracious and informative. The neat, organized shelving displays a splendid selection of East Indian dals, grains, legumes, spices, herbs and specialty foods for very competitive prices. If you are in town, J.B. Foods is well worth a visit: 6607 Main St., Vancouver, B.C.

K

KTC CREAMED COCONUT. Creamed coconut usually comes as a 200 g (7.05 oz) brick, wrapped in wax paper and placed in a cardboard box. If you plan to grate the creamed coconut, the job is made easier by refrigerating the block beforehand. (If making cream or milk, grating is not necessary. Simply break the block into a bowl and add warm water in the amounts of 450 or 600 mL respectively. Stir until dissolved.) There are several brands which are quite usable, but in some I have found the texture inconsistent, the color off-white, and occasionally the odor rancid. Over the years I have found the KTC brand to be the most reliable for quality, but it is not my purpose to dissuade you from trying others.

M

MANGO POWDER is obtainable in ethnic grocery stores, especially East Indian.

MCT (MEDIUM CHAIN TRIGLYCERIDE) oil. For background information on this product see Chapter Two, *Coconuts and Health*. The product can be difficult to find in grocery and health food stores. If you reach a dead-end with retail enquiries, I suggest you write direct to Sound Nutrition, Inc. to order bottles of their ThinOil™. The address is P.O. Box 555, Dover, ID, U.S.A. 83825, or call 1-800-THINOIL. They will ship if you purchase a whole carton (twelve bottles).

N

NORI. Since sushi dishes have become so popular, nori, the sticky-rice wrap, should be in your regular grocery store—unless you live in an exceptionally small community. Ask your store's manager to stock it: other shoppers will be grateful!

O

OMEGA NUTRITION CANADA INC. is described in Chapter Two, *Coconuts and Health,* as well as listed under 'Coconut oil' above. This company produces organic oils which are nothing short of excellent. It has relocated to 1695 Franklin Street, Vancouver, BC, Canada, V5L 1P5. Mail orders welcomed: tel. 1-800-661-3529 or fax. 1-604-253-4228.

P

PRUNE PUREE. There are several brands available. My favorite is Just Like Shortening, available at health food stores and the more sophisticated supermarkets. Similar emulsions of fruits and vegetables are on the market. Among these I recommend WonderSlim, but find it best for sauces and flourless baking. The Community Food Co-op in Bellingham, WA, has large supplies. (For details see under 'Community' above.)

PURE COCOA POWDER is to be distinguished from hot chocolate mix which has a variety of additives. Any brand will suit the recipes in this book. WonderSlim is recommended as the company produces a pure, low-fat (extracted by mechanical pressing) cocoa powder with no preservatives, artificial coloring or flavoring. Available in health food stores and the larger supermarkets.

S

SOUR-SOP, also known as 'guanabana,' is a large, unprepossessing fruit covered with softish thorns. Its pulp has a refreshing, slightly acidic taste. In Hawaii it is everywhere. In Canada it is to be found in the freezer section of stores selling sub-tropical edibles. The 'Caribbean' (see above) always stocks it. Typically, it comes in 60 g sachets, eight to a box.

SOY MILK is located in the dietary section of most grocery outlets.

U

UBE FLOUR (or powdered ube) is from a Philippine variety of yam. This product is often available in ethnic markets, the innovative delicatessen and, of course, the Caribbean & Newfoundland Market. See above.

UWAJIMAYA INC.: a marvellous Japanese department store south of the border. From books to furniture to imported foods, it boasts a fine collection of fresh and dried sea-vegetables (seaweeds). Reminder: not all the fresh varieties are always in season. The store is open daily from 9 a.m. to 8 p.m. The address is 519 6th Avenue, Seattle, WA, U.S.A., 98104. Tel. 206-624-6248. Fax 206-624-6915. Yes, they do mail orders, and yes, they respond to written, phoned and faxed enquiries.

INDEX